The Wormhaven Gardening Book: Understanding God's Six Day Creation Can Make Gardening Easy, Fun, Inexpensive, Healthy and Educational for the Whole Family

Pastor Gregory L. Jackson, Ph. D.

Illustrated by
James B. Romnes

Martin Chemnitz Press
22 N. State Street
New Ulm, Minnesota 56073

The Wormhaven Gardening Book: Understanding God's Six Day Creation Can Make Gardening Easy, Fun, Inexpensive, Healthy and Educational for the Whole Family

Library of Congress Card 96-086580
Pastor Gregory L. Jackson, Ph. D.
22 N. State Street
New Ulm, MN 56703
Published 1996
Printed in the United States of America,
Morris Publishing, Kearney, NE
ISBN 0-9649354-3-0

Table of Contents

Introduction

"The spirit of the worm beneath the sod In love and worship, blends itself with God." *Epipsychidion*, by Percy Bysshe Shelley

Many people find their first efforts at gardening to be fruitless, or the labor and cost so great that one would rather pursue a saner hobby, such as base jumping or restoring Studebakers. My first effort in the 1980s resulted in weeds which appeared less than vigorous. A local wit said, "The best looking thing in your garden is that dead bird lying on the ground."

Humbled but not defeated, I resolved to learn as much as possible and to experiment as I studied. I had the good fortune to have an excellent library in Midland, Michigan, as well as the advice of a herbalist, chemists, and chemical engineers. I wanted to find some basic principles which would explain the natural world and make gardening appealing to novices and to children. How can we get the right chemicals to the plants, supply enough water, reduce the weeds, defeat harmful insects, and produce nutritious food and stunning flowers without using manmade toxins?

My interest in gardening grew with my alarm at the state of Christianity in America. I came to realize that the older or mainline denominations, generally associated with the National and World Council of Churches, were opponents of the basic doctrines of the Christian faith, from the inerrancy of Scriptures to the resurrection of Christ. The liberal denominations were likely to go to court against the teaching of Creation in the schools while arguing in favor of evolution, boasting about the lawsuits in their periodicals. The more I learned about gardening, the more I saw how every aspect of nature played a specific role in God's design and purpose.

The key issues in gardening are pivotal in Christianity as well:
1) evolution or Six Day Creation,
2) the power and effectiveness of the Word,
3) the proper use of reason.

When we have a clearer understanding of Creation, all other doctrines also mean more to us. This would be true if we started with any other doctrine, since all articles of faith are really part of one unified whole: the Gospel of Jesus Christ, the Son of God. One doctrine leads to another, and if one is no longer held as taught by God's Word, then all doctrines will fall in time. Thus we have in all the older denominations

a collapse of faith which is unprecedented in scope but predicted in the Scriptures.

> For the time will come when they will not endure sound doctrine; but after their own lusts shall they heap to themselves teachers, having itching ears; {4} And they shall turn away their ears from the truth, and shall be turned unto fables. (2 Timothy 4:3-4)

> Now the Spirit speaketh expressly, that in the latter times some shall depart from the faith, giving heed to seducing spirits, and doctrines of devils; {2} Speaking lies in hypocrisy; having their conscience seared with a hot iron....(1 Timothy 4:1-2)

Our nation has suffered greatly from abandoning the assumption of the Declaration of Independence, natural law, that right and wrong are based on divine Creation. When we were closer to the soil, we were also closer to the One who created the soil.

The first version of *The Wormhaven Gardening Book* was read and enjoyed by the faculty of Wisconsin Lutheran Seminary, who asked to have a copy catalogued and placed in the library. Since then, Bill and Martha Blumenschein have continuously asked, "When is that gardening book coming out?" Others have asked about it, read it, and urged it to be published. One gardener said, "Whenever I see an earthworm, I think of you, Pastor Jackson." Ken and Joan Nissing said that the manuscript changed their attitude about pests. Pastor Herman Otten read the manuscript and mulched his newly planted trees with leftover copies of *Christian News*. The book began as letters to our dear friends, Leroy and Eleanor Alexander, and evolved from there. I was lucky to have James Romnes agree to draw for the book, since he illustrates Creation principles with a keen sense of humor. The first Creation lecture I attended was given by Dr. David Menton, an anatomy professor at Washington University School of Medicine and a member of the Church of the Lutheran Confession, a denomination I recently joined. To all our friends who laughed when I picked up a shovel and who dropped by later for perfect sweet corn, this book is affectionately dedicated.

Creation

Science will never prove to anyone that God created the universe in six days. Human reason does not have the power to convert someone to faith. Only the Word of God can create faith, because God has bound Himself to the Word, not due to any lack or limitation, but solely through His gracious will. Therefore, the Holy Spirit always works through the Word and never apart from the Word. For that reason, we can always be confident that God is at work when the Word is proclaimed, read, or remembered. We also know that no human can improve on God's Word or bring to life that which quickens the dead in their tombs, heals leprosy, stills storms, turns water into wine, converts the dead sinner into a new life in Christ, and preserves the believer for eternal life through the Word.

> Let the wicked forsake his way, and the unrighteous man his thoughts: and let him return unto the LORD, and he will have mercy upon him; and to our God, for he will abundantly pardon. {8} For my thoughts are not your thoughts, neither are your ways my ways, saith the LORD. {9} For as the heavens are higher than the earth, so are my ways higher than your ways, and my thoughts than your thoughts. {10} For as the rain cometh down, and the snow from heaven, and returneth not thither, but watereth the earth, and maketh it bring forth and bud, that it may give seed to the sower, and bread to the eater: {11} So shall my word be that goeth forth out of my mouth: it shall not return unto me void, but it shall accomplish that which I please, and it shall prosper in the thing whereto I sent it. (Isaiah 55:7-11)

God is telling us through Isaiah that His Word is always efficacious, or effective, at work, energetic in accomplishing His will.

If we understand the crucial passage in Isaiah, then the Creation is not a theory to be proved with human reason but the revelation of God, to be served by human reason. This is a crucial distinction for Christians. If we place human reason above the Scriptures, then human judgment will ultimately reject the Word, because "My thoughts are not your thoughts." Placing human reason above the Word is called the magisterial use of reason, because it makes reason the teacher or master (*magister*, Latin for teacher). Even if we only try to make the

Scriptures reasonable or attractive, we are still falling under the spell of Uncle Fred, our human reason, which will never be completely satisfied. We all have an Uncle Fred, who will say, after hours of fact-studded argument, "You still haven't convinced me!" The Bible is the Word of God, even if no one in the entire world believes it.

The most brilliant minds have already learned that all the archeological facts in the Bible are completely true, even down to minor details. The very doubts which were used in the past to hold the Bible up to ridicule, such as the existence of the Hittites or Ninevah, are now known to be quashed by undeniable physical evidence. We have never had so many facts about the Biblical lands nor so much doubt expressed by the ordained professors of mainline seminaries. Facts do not convert

because they lack the power inherent in the Word of God.

Far better to ask theological questions about the facts of science. Charles Darwin spent 40 years studying earthworms and wrote a definitive book based on his careful observations. Two questions remain unanswered in his classic work, and they nag at every scientific observation of our universe, from the star-ripping black hole of Cygnus to the microscopic springtails of the compost pit.

The first question is that of purpose. Science cannot answer this question, which grows ever more complex when pursued. Flowers feed bees with pollen and nectar. Bees pollinate. Flowers and bees need each other. Why does this happen? Every creature has a purpose, and each purpose is linked together into one vast ecosystem which is, in turn, linked with the sun, moon, and forces which we barely understand. Evolution meanders along the path of "how?," with assumptions about random events happening over enormous stretches of time, but the best evolution scheme fails to address "why?"

The second question is that of design. No matter how often a person talks about evolution, he is often stuck with the word design. For instance, a TV show on sharks described them as "suddenly appearing" in evolution as "perfectly designed killing machines." The perfect design must have a perfect Designer.

> For every house is builded by some man; but he that built all things is God. (Hebrews 3:4)

If I wanted an evolutionist to believe in Creation, I would ask questions about purpose and design until all his explanations became unhinged. Then I would tell him what the inerrant Bible teaches: that creatures were created for a purpose.

A. Through the Word

The purpose of the Bible is to bring about faith in Christ Jesus:

> But these are written, that ye might believe that Jesus is the Christ, the Son of God; and that believing ye might have life through his name. (John 20:31)

The Bible has no other purpose, although it contains a wealth of information about history and examples of beautiful poetry. The Bible does not serve to satisfy curiosity but to call people into the Kingdom of God through the "engrafted Word, which is able to save your souls." (James 1:21)

The Bible is Christ-centered, so the Six Day Creation of the universe in Genesis 1 is welded to Christ as the creating Word in John 1, and to St. Paul's passages about the believer being a new creature.

> Therefore if any man be in Christ, he is a new creature: old things are passed away; behold, all things are become new. (2 Corinthians 5:17)

> For in Christ Jesus neither circumcision availeth any thing, nor uncircumcision, but a new creature. (Galatians 6:15)

The power of God is expressed in His Word. When He speaks, the earth melts (Psalm 46:6) and the mountains skip like rams (Psalm 114:6). The universe was created by God's command, in six days.

Creation Out of Nothing (ex nihilo)

In the beginning God created the heaven and the earth. {2} And the earth was without form, and void; and darkness was upon the face of the deep. And the Spirit of God moved upon the face of the waters. (Genesis 1:1-2)

First Day

{3} And God said, Let there be light: and there was light. {4} And God saw the light, that it was good: and God divided the light from the darkness. {5} And God called the light Day, and the darkness he called Night. And the evening and the morning were the first day.

Second Day

{6} And God said, Let there be a firmament in the midst of the waters, and let it divide the waters from the waters. {7} And God made the firmament, and divided the waters which were under the firmament from the waters which were above the firmament: and it was so. {8} And God called the firmament Heaven. And the evening and the morning were the second day.

Third Day

{9} And God said, Let the waters under the heaven be gathered together unto one place, and let the dry land appear: and it was so. {10} And God called the dry land Earth; and the gathering together of the waters called he Seas: and God saw that it was good. {11} And God said, Let the earth bring forth grass, the herb yielding seed, and the fruit tree yielding fruit after his kind, whose seed is in itself, upon the earth: and it was so. {12} And the earth brought forth grass, and herb yielding seed after his kind, and the tree yielding fruit, whose seed was in itself, after his kind: and God saw that it was good. {13} And the evening and the morning were the third day.

Fourth Day

{14} And God said, Let there be lights in the firmament of the heaven to divide the day from the night; and let them be for signs, and for seasons, and for days, and years: {15} And let them be for lights in the firmament of the heaven to give light upon the earth: and it was so. {16} And God made two great lights; the greater light to rule the day, and the lesser light to rule the night: he made the stars also. {17} And God set them in the firmament of the heaven to give light upon the earth, {18} And to rule over the day and over the night, and to divide the light from the darkness: and God saw that it was good. {19} And the evening and the morning were the fourth day.

Fifth Day

{20} And God said, Let the waters bring forth abundantly the moving creature that hath life, and fowl that may fly above the earth in the open firmament of heaven. {21} And God created great whales, and every living creature that moveth, which the waters brought forth abundantly, after their kind, and every winged fowl after his kind: and God saw that it was good. {22} And God blessed them, saying, Be fruitful, and multiply, and fill the waters in the seas, and let fowl multiply in the earth. {23} And the evening and the morning were the fifth day.

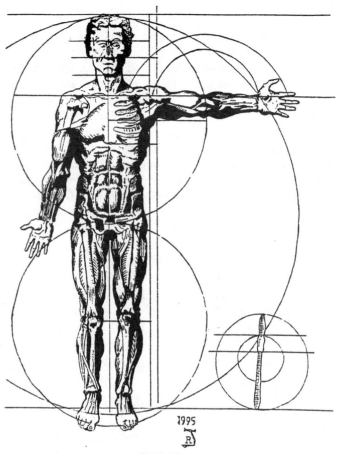

1995

Sixth Day

{24} And God said, Let the earth bring forth the living creature after his kind, cattle, and creeping thing, and beast of the earth after his kind: and it was so. {25} And God made the beast of the earth after his kind, and cattle after their kind, and every thing that creepeth upon the earth after his kind: and God saw that it was good. {26} And God said, Let us make man in our image, after our likeness: and let them have dominion over the fish of the sea, and over the fowl of the air, and over the cattle, and over all the earth, and over every creeping thing that creepeth upon the earth. {27} So God created man in his own image, in the image of God created he him; male and female created he them. {28} And God blessed them, and God said unto them, Be fruitful, and multiply, and replenish the earth, and subdue it: and have dominion over the fish of the sea, and over the fowl of the air, and over every living thing that moveth upon the earth. {29} And God said, Behold, I have given you every herb bearing seed, which is upon the face of all the earth, and every tree, in the which is the fruit of a tree yielding seed; to you it shall be for meat. {30} And to every beast of the earth, and to every fowl of the air, and to every thing that creepeth upon the earth, wherein there is life, I have given every green herb for meat: and it was so. {31} And God saw every thing that he had made, and, behold, it was very good. And the evening and the morning were the sixth day.

Seventh Day

Thus the heavens and the earth were finished, and all the host of them. {2} And on the seventh day God ended his work which he had made; and he rested on the seventh day from all his work which he had made. {3} And God blessed the seventh day, and sanctified it: because that in it he had rested from all his work which God created and made. (Genesis 2:1-3)

Some 19th century Christian leaders tried to compromise with the fad of evolution making God the power behind the multi-billion year development of organic compounds into man—as if God needed the time to accomplish so great a work. The result of placing reason above Scripture was the ultimate rejection of any form of Creation and the advocacy of evolution by the mainline denominations, who proudly go to court on behalf of Charles Darwin's theory today.

In contrast, the ministerial use of reason makes the mind a humble servant of the Word, because: "My thoughts are not your thoughts, neither are your ways my ways, saith the LORD. {9} For as the heavens are higher than the earth, so are my ways higher than your ways, and my thoughts than your thoughts." (Isaiah 55:8-9) This does not mean advocating ignorance or anti-intellectualism, but using all our God-given powers to make clear what He reveals to us in His Word.

Denying Creation is the same as denying Christ, for: "All things were made by him; and without him was not any thing made that was made." (John 1:3) Because Jesus was present at Creation as the Word of God, every single living and inanimate thing in our world and all the vast expanse of the heavens are touched and shaped by Him. Every-thing which delights man has come from God, and the evidence for God's Creation is all around us, leaving us no excuse to doubt His Creation. Paul's speech on Mars' hill was based upon a universal concept of Creation, even if pagans misunderstood the nature of God.

God that made the world and all things therein, seeing that he is Lord of heaven and earth, dwelleth not in temples made with hands; {25} Neither is worshipped with men's hands, as though he needed any thing, seeing he giveth to all life, and breath, and all things; {26} And hath made of one blood all nations of men for to dwell on all the face of the earth, and hath determined the times before appointed, and the bounds of their habitation; {27} That they should seek the Lord, if haply they might feel after him, and find him, though he be not far from every one of us: {28} For in him we live, and move, and have our being; as certain also of your own poets have said, For we are also his offspring. (Acts 17:24-28)

When Paul wrote to the Romans, his inspired words about salvation in Christ were connected directly with Creation.

For I am not ashamed of the gospel of Christ: for it is the power of God unto salvation to every one that believeth; to the Jew first, and also to the Greek. For therein is the righteousness of God revealed from faith to faith: as it is written, The just shall live by faith. {18} For the wrath of God is revealed from heaven against all ungodliness and unrighteousness of men, who hold the truth in unrighteousness; {19} Because that which may be known of God is manifest in them; for God hath showed it unto them. {20} For the invisible things of him from the creation of the world are clearly seen, being understood by the things that are made, even his eternal power and Godhead; so that they are without excuse: {21} Because that, when they knew God, they glorified him not as God, neither were thankful; but became vain in their imaginations, and their foolish heart was darkened. (Romans 1:16-21)

Our sinful nature, inherited from Adam, makes us imagine we can make ourselves pleasing to God through works. But the Holy Spirit works through the Law to show us our wretched state without God. When the Law brings us to contrition by pounding our hardened hearts into pieces and burning away our impurities (Jeremiah 23:29), we are eager to hear how Christ died on the cross for our sins, won forgiveness and eternal life for us, defeated Satan, and rose victorious from the dead.

The doctrine of Creation is not argued in the Bible, but stated throughout.

> Praise him, ye heavens of heavens, and ye waters that be above the heavens. Let them praise the name of the LORD: for he commanded, and they were created. (Psalm 148:4-5)

The knowledge of Creation which is given to every believer through faith, is the foundation for our confidence in God's power and His purpose. Nothing is impossible for the Creator.

> Hast thou not known? hast thou not heard, that the everlasting God, the LORD, the Creator of the ends of the earth, fainteth not, neither is weary? there is no searching of his understanding. {29} He giveth power to the faint; and to them that have no might he increaseth strength. {30} Even the youths shall faint and be weary, and the young men shall utterly fall: {31} But they that wait upon the LORD shall renew their strength; they shall mount up with wings as eagles; they shall run, and not be weary; and they shall walk, and not faint. (Isaiah 40:28-31)

When we consider how much God has done and will do for us, through His Word, then all the doubts about His Creation fade in significance. And when we consider how finely tuned His created world is, from the lunar tides to the complex functions of each cell, our faith in His love for each and every one of us grows as we see it revealed time after time in His inerrant Word.

ONE

The Earthworm in the Garden

"A man may fish with the worm that hath eat of a king, and eat of the fish that hath fed of that worm." William Shakespeare, *Hamlet*, IV, 3, 29

The earthworm belongs to the phylum annelida (rings of muscle; Latin, *annellus*, ring), the class chaetopoda (meaning bristle-footed), and the order oligochaeta (few bristles). Some earthworms worth knowing are:

Lumbricus terrestris

The nightcrawler, dew worm, or rain worm, a deep digger with permanent tunnels, harvested at night from lawns, difficult to breed commercially.

Allolobophora caliginosa

The field (orchard, grey, brown) worm, larger than a red wiggler and smaller than a nightcrawler, works in the top foot of soil, more tolerant of mediocre soil than the red wiggler. Based on his research, Andre Voisin thinks very highly of the field worm's ability to improve soil.

L. rubellus	The red worm or red wiggler, a small and active digger in the top foot of soil, a prolific breeder, a fishing worm which wiggles under water.
Eisenia foetida	The manure worm or red-gold hybrid, ringed with yellow and maroon, a great breeder with an odor problem, loves rich soil and manure piles. This guy can be used to compost garbage in a pail in the home.
Pheretima	Swamp worm (from India) now found in America, very active, lashes around when held in the fingers.
Megascolides Australis	Australian earthworm, up to eleven feet long, large enough to capture Moby Dick with a very large fishing pole.

The first two worms are most likely to be found in anyone's yard. People introduce the red wiggler into the yard by buying 1000 for $10-12 and placing them in areas where they are most likely to thrive: in compost, in manure, or in rich soil. Red wigglers will improve the soil quickly, but they require good soil which is already rich in organic matter.

The purpose of *The Wormhaven Gardening Book* is to harness the power of God's Six Day Creation, which will make gardening easy, fun, inexpensive, healthy, and instructive for the family. Veteran gardeners will find some of their theories confirmed, and others exploded, depending on how close to the soil they are.

One could speak about Creation by pointing out the power we see revealed in the starry skies, but most do not have access to telescopes, binoculars, or clear dark skies. Astronomy is a fascinating hobby which makes one say with the Psalmist: "The heavens declare the glory of God; and the firmament showeth his handiwork." (Psalms 19:1) But to view a given object, such as the nebula in Orion's belt, one must have the right weather, the right season, the right clothes, the right telescopic instrument, and a lack of social responsibilities. To enjoy the nearest wonders of Creation, one only needs a set of eyes and ears.

The Earthworm in the Garden

Many gardening books frighten the beginner by suggesting the use of expensive tools and aids, such as rototillers, fertilizers, pesticides, and special gadgets. Other books alarm the reader with backbreaking advice on double digging, trenching, and similar techniques. Still others confuse the would-be gardener with esoteric names, soil analysis, and cryptic numbers (5-10-5). Unfortunately, even the best books miss the essential ingredient for a flourishing garden: the earthworm, a creature designed specifically by God to make the soil productive.

Several important gardening books have touched upon the crucial nature of the earthworm's work in making soil productive. Edward Faulkner's *Plowman's Folly* questioned the whole matter of plowing or digging up soil. He argued convincingly that plowing has continued mostly as a tradition rather than as a method of soil improvement. Using cover crops on unproductive soil, Faulkner was able to show that compacted soil could become fertile without plowing. Today his theories are supported by the widespread use of no-till farming.

Ruth Stout's *How to Have a Green Thumb Without an Aching Back* showed that her heavily mulched garden never required weeding or tilling. Soil scientists noted that her soil was full of earthworms.

Wilfred Edward Shewall-Cooper's *Compost Gardening* also argued for the no-dig method of gardening, showing that the earthworms will pull down all the compost laid on the top of the soil. The compost serves as a weed barrier, a mulch to conserve moisture, and as food for the plants via the digestive system of the earthworms.

Those who know and love the lowly earthworm will immediately recognize one thing all three books have in common—their ideas lead to prolific earthworm production. Cover crops provide humus (organic matter) for earthworms, allowing them to multiply and break up hardpan soil. Mulching with plant material not only adds humus but also keeps the soil moist, dark, and cool for the earthworms. Compost provides even better food for the earthworms, since it is digested humus, plus the advantage of earthworm egg capsule distribution. In contrast, many common techniques are harmful to the earthworm: rototilling, overuse of inorganic fertilizers and pesticides, leaving the soil bare between plants, throwing away garden refuse and weeds.

Have people stopped to wonder why certain methods work only a short time, while others succeed year after year? If manure is so good for soil, why does nothing grow on a manure pile, while compost piles accidentally grow perfect plants? Why are some areas of the globe fertile, while others are unproductive? Why is America threatened with another Dust Bowl experience? Tragically, most people do not understand how all of God's Creation works together. While nature shows flourish on the cable channels and the networks, seldom will one hear the Creator given credit for all the wonders upon which the television show dwells.

One documentary announced that birds evolved from lizards, without showing that birds have very specialized organs required for flight, with no anatomical parallels in the lizards: eyes, lungs, bones, digestion. The bird feather, necessary for flight, is a "miracle," said the announcer, without blushing. Dr. David Menton's lecture on the bird feather shows with microscopic slides that the feather is kept in shape by a velcro like system which matches tiny hooks with tiny grooves, billions of them in a single bird. The design is so delicate and orderly that greater magnification only makes people gasp even more. Dr. Menton says, "Man-made objects, such as a Swiss watch, look worse and worse under magnification, because the flaws show up. In God's Creation, every plant and animal looks more and more impressive and complex when we look closer and closer. It's just like the ad, the closer you look, the better Creation looks."

We do not spend much time thinking about the special nature of bird anatomy, which seems so obvious, since flight dictates these structures. The desire to fly does not create or change anatomical structure, so each feature must be designed by God.

> And God said, Let the waters bring forth abundantly the moving creature that hath life, and fowl that may fly above the earth in the open firmament of heaven. {21} And God created great whales, and every living creature that moveth, which the waters brought forth abundantly, after their kind, and every winged fowl after his kind: and God saw that it was good. {22} And God blessed them, saying, Be fruitful, and multiply, and fill the waters in the seas, and let fowl multiply in the earth. (Genesis 1:20-22)

God does not tell us how He designed birds for flight in Genesis, but He gave us the ability to learn and to marvel, to long for the freedom and mobility of the bird in flight.

The earthworm is no less a miracle than a bird in flight, but not an object of our envy, since no one wants to crawl in the dirt in abject humility.

The nations shall see and be confounded at all their might: they shall lay their hand upon their mouth, their ears shall be deaf. They shall lick the dust like a serpent, they shall move out of their holes like worms of the earth: they shall be afraid of the LORD our God, and shall fear because of thee.   (Micah 7:16-17)

Yet the sinless Son of God became sin, a worm, dying on the cross for our sins, fulfilling the Messianic prophesy of Psalm 22:6: "But I am a worm, and no man; a reproach of men, and despised of the people."

The earthworm is a common creature, occupying our lawns and farms by the millions, turning up under rocks and fallen branches, found beneath every pile of leaves, coiled around a dandelion root pulled from the grass, hiding between the soil and a bunch of newspapers carelessly tossed on the ground. Because it's so common, therefore, people seldom think of the earthworm as a marvel of God's Creation, a perfectly designed

Sure, the Hanging Gardens are nice but what a commute!

earthmoving machine, a machine which modifies and improves the soil it moves. Far less do they realize that our lives revolve around the earthworm, since the productivity of the soil depends upon the earthworm, who will feed us as well as we feed him.

Argumentative people will say that the earthworm is necessary but not sufficient for a successful garden. One must also have adequate soil, moisture, birds, and sunshine. Nor does the earthworm work alone in the soil. A host of insects, bacteria, molds, and mammals add to the earthworm's vast contribution. An earthworm would be the first to say, "No worm is an island, each to his own..."

The earthworm is really a synecdoche, a part standing for the whole, as a ship represents the navy. However, by making the earthworm a superstar, gardeners can utilize the ecology of the entire property and neighborhood resources, with mutual benefits derived not only from Creation but also from one's neighbors. The results for me have been: remarkable productivity at a low cost of money and time, closer neighborhood ties, healthy food in abundance, exercise, and a new appreciation of God's purpose and design in nature.

Most people think of earthworms as totally tubular creatures which wait in the ground for robins and fishermen. I had no appreciation of them when I first attempted serious gardening in 1981. As I started to read about gardening and nature at the Grace Dow Public Library in Midland, Michigan, I found that one can hardly separate the plant growing in the garden from its surroundings. Soil, trees, walls, fences, birds, pets, rainfall, pests, shrubs, sunshine, and weeds all contribute to the final equation.

Convinced that the earthworm was the key component in promoting soil fertility, I determined to garden in such a way that the earthworm would be fruitful and multiply, sharing its blessings with me by plowing the earth day and night, opening up the soil for air and rain to penetrate, fertilizing the soil with its castings, pulling organic matter into the earth, and sweetening the soil with its calciferous glands. Therefore, I have called our gardens Wormhaven. Wormhaven.1 thrived at our parsonage in Midland, Michigan. Wormhaven.2 was filled with roses at our parsonage in Columbus, Ohio. Wormhaven.3 is at our Church of the Lutheran Confession parsonage in New Ulm, Minnesota.

THE WORMHAVEN THESES
(after Luther)
or
The Diet of Worms

1. According to God's design and purpose, the active earthworms (lumbricids) are the primary cause of soil fertility, as indicated by the Nile River Delta, the migration of lumbricids to America, and the transformation of the soil in New Zealand in recent times.

2. The value of manure, compost and mulch in improving soil fertility comes mainly from organic material causing the increased activity of the earthworm in aerating, mixing, humifying, and fertilizing the soil. (Humify means to add humus to the soil.)

3. Earthworms are the most important (but not the only) soil creatures designed by God to benefit the gardener. Soil fertility depends on the combined effects of bacteria, molds, insects, arthropods, and earthworms.

4. Creating an environment favorable for plant growth will invariably favor the earthworm, whether it be composting, mulching, or watering. At the same time, other animal life will flourish, both prey and predators. Pests will attract predators and be minimized.

5. The environment favorable to earthworms is different from most assumptions about agriculture. Earthworms favor the trashy look rather than bare soil, organic matter rather than inorganic fertilizers, peace rather than plowing and tilling, natural controls rather than manufactured toxins.

6. Healthy soil and healthy earthworms are mutually sustaining, each requiring the other. Healthy plant life results from this symbiosis, which involves a host of organisms. As decreed by God, man benefits from this relationship by eating healthy food and promotes this relationship by his stewardship of God's Creation.

So God created man in his own image, in the image of God created he him; male and female created he them. {28} And God blessed them, and God said unto them, Be fruitful, and multiply, and replenish the earth, and subdue it: and have dominion over the fish of the sea, and over the fowl of the air, and over every living thing that moveth upon the earth. {29} And God said, Behold, I have given you every herb bearing seed, which is upon the face have given you every herb bearing seed, which is upon the face of all the earth, and every tree, in the which is the fruit of a tree yielding seed; to you it shall be for meat. {30} And to every beast of the earth, and to every fowl of the air, and to every thing that creepeth upon the earth, wherein there is life, I have given every green herb for meat: and it was so. {31} And God saw every thing that he had made, and, behold, it was very good. (Genesis 1:27-31)

7. Weeds and earthworms naturally renew soil. Weeds hold soil in place while creating humus and passageways for earthworms. Later, the site improves enough to allow more desirable plants to survive. Weeds also benefit the soil by attracting beneficial insects and birds, which combine to suppress harmful insects.

8. Cover crops or green manure help the soil by creating humus for earthworms, holding the soil in place, and breaking up hard soil.

THE BIOLOGY OF EARTHWORMS

The Quest for the Historical Earthworm

The ancient Egyptians knew the value of the earthworm, whose lifestyle was intimately connected with the well-known seasonal flooding of the Nile River. The ancient Egyptians were not permitted to take a single earthworm from their country, and farmers were not allowed to touch them, lest they offend the god of fertility.[1] Cleopatra declared them to be sacred, which indicates her respect for worms.[2]

The ancient people were far more observant than we have proved to be. The advent of the scientific age provided the impetus to study the cause of the Nile's fertility, which would not be explained by seasonal flooding alone. The British government's investigation, summarized by Barrett, gives a large part of the credit to the earthworm, which takes advantage of the opportunities provided by nature.

The rainy season of the Nile Valley begins in June of each year, turning the Nile into a swift, silt-laden torrent. The silt comprises 17 percent of the river water and is itself made up of half mineral and half organic matter. When this soup enters the lowland of Gesira after a 500-mile journey, it spreads out across 9,000 miles of irrigation channels.

The tunneling activity of the earthworm allows the water to infiltrate the soil rapidly, leaving behind, on the surface, a rich top-dressing of organic and mineral matter, ideal food for the earthworm. The dense population of earthworms turns the food into 120 tons of castings per acre during the six month growing season. These castings (a polite term for excrement) are the finest type of natural fertilizer available. The tunneling keeps the soil loose, aerated, and capable of holding moisture. When the soil dries out and earthworms die, their nitrogen rich bodies provide a final boost of fertility for the soil. The Egyptians wisely connected earthworm abundance with soil productivity. For 40 centuries the Egyptians maintained a superior civilization, based upon their superb agriculture and their exaltation of the earthworm.[3]

If the earthworm is the key to Egypt's phenomenal success, why then has the rest of the world lagged behind in agriculture, since each country has water, earthworms, and a need for plentiful food? The answer may lie with the unfortunate truth that all earthworms are not created equal. The taxonomy of earthworms may not be very interesting to the typical gardener, but most have noticed that some earthworms are much bigger than others.

Almost all American earthworms belong to the family of Lumbricidae (Latin, *lumbricus*, worm), but we cannot take credit for them. Like many of us, they are descended from the immigrants who first came to America from Europe. Our relatives came by boat, but the earthworms' came by shoe, hoof, and plant. Lumbricids have proved to be as hard working as their human counterparts, imbued with the lumbricoid version of the Protestant Work Ethic. Their efforts have turned America's fertile soil into productive soil, just as they did with Egypt's, according to one theory.

Andre Voisin argues in *Better Grassland Sward* that the earth had only a narrow band of territory where the active Lumbricids could be found: the Indus, Euphrates, and Nile valleys.[4] These were the areas where some of the greatest civilizations started and flourished. Yale University's E. Huntington has shown in *Mainsprings of Civilization* that many areas of the world did not develop until they were colonized by Europeans. Areas of high potential which developed after colonization were: the mouth of the Rio de la Plata in South America; large sections of the United States; an area of southern Africa; the southeastern tip of Australia, and all of New Zealand.[5] New Zealand provides the best test case, because farmers remember a time when the soil barely supported plant life.

In 1925, a New Zealand farmer began to inoculate his soil with earthworms from Europe and productivity increased as they spread. He owned 875 acres of "poor, wild pasture." He dug up clumps of soil and vegetation from rich soil where earthworms were active and planted them randomly in the poor soil. He continued this work from 1925-1945. The results were impressive:

> By this time, although all the other conditions remained the same, *the change in the flora was striking*. The poor hill pastures that had formerly comprised brown top and *Danthonia* (poverty grass, a species found on poor soils) were now transformed into rye-grass-dominant swards. Stocking rates and yields per acre had increased enormously parallel to this improvement in composition.[6]

We understand from the geologists that the last Ice Age removed earthworms from the northern part of the United States entirely. Another consideration would be the effect of the global flood. Colonists brought earthworms over with their plants and livestock, inadvertently promoting the fertility they sought in the new land.

What are the Lubricids which have done so much for civilization?
1.   The best known is the common nightcrawler or dew worm (*Lumbricus terrestris*), known for mating, feeding, and depositing its casts above ground at night or on rainy days. Nightcrawlers can burrow up to 15 feet, breaking up subsoil. Nightcrawlers are often sold as bait for fishermen, but they are usually harvested from lawns rather than bred commercially. Their deep digging habits makes them want to leave the shallow boxes where most worms are bred.
2.   A popular commercial worm is the red wiggler (*Lumbricus rubellus*; Latin, *rubellus*, red). The five-inch red wiggler looks rather dainty next to the nightcrawler, which can reach a foot in length. Red wigglers are famous for their prolific breeding habits and their ability to turn organic material quickly into compost, if conditions are right.
3.   Manure worms (*Eisenia foetida*) are known for their bad smell when stepped on and for their yellow and maroon coloration. They are also prolific breeders who require a high level of organic materials to sustain

life. Needless to say, they are often found near manure piles.

4.   The common field worm (*Allolobophora caliginosa*) is often dug up by gardeners during the day. A nightcrawler withdraws from the vibration of digging, so he will not be in a shovel of dirt. Red wigglers are easily distinguished by their color and are less likely to be found in a yard or field unless introduced there. A worm which lashes from side to side when held in the fingers is likely to be a *Pheretima* from India and Eastern Asia. All these came over on the Mayflower, or a little later, adding America to the list of great civilizations sustained by agriculture.

The digression on the identification of earthworms may have left some gardeners impatiently hoping for useful material rather than the quest for the historical earthworm. Sadly, all earthworms have been lumped together. Even in the "Scientific Age," the famous Charles Darwin failed to identify the species he studied for 40 years. Worst of all, the earthworm has not received half the careful study given the loathsome cockroach or the useless louse. In fact, Darwin's study was especially damaging for two reasons. First of all, he was so thorough in some respects that he reduced the need for another earthworm study. Secondly, he missed the agricultural applications when the world was poised to pursue the pursuit of better farming through chemistry.

Organic gardeners use the date of 1840 to mark the beginning of the Babylonian Captivity of the Soil, for in that year Justus von Liebig published his *Chemistry of Agriculture and Physiology*, which showed that plants obtain their food from basic chemicals such as nitrogen, phosphorous, and potassium (N-P-K in bags of fertilizer). Before the textbook was published, the humus theory prevailed, which held that organic material in the soil made the soil more productive. Afterwards, scientific agriculture grew rapidly in the optimistic century of technological advances in every area of life.

No wonder that Darwin's little book, *The Formation of Vegetable Mould Through the Action of Worms*, (published in 1881, after he had become famous for his *Origin of Species*), was overlooked by the general population. Darwin was one of the first to show that all soil eventually passes through the earthworm's body. With singular eloquence he concluded his study:

> The plough is one of the most ancient and most valuable of man's inventions; but long before he existed the land was in fact regularly ploughed, and still continues to be thus ploughed by earthworms. It may be doubted whether there are many other

animals which have played so important a part in the history of the world, as have these lowly organized creatures.[7]

Nevertheless, this small classic was largely ignored, except by what we might call the earthworm community. Darwin missed the whole point of why God created the earthworm: while he carefully analyzed how earthworms gradually bury all of man's buildings, he failed to see how they improved the soil. Darwin is a perfect example of liberals who observe and record with excruciating exactness, only to arrive at all the wrong conclusions from the facts.

Agriculture moved rapidly into manufactured fertilizer and later into pesticides, but a few unknowns saw the value of God's design. Barrett's *Harnessing the Earthworm* reveals that George Sheffield Oliver's grandfather had one of the first wormhaven farms, in operation from 1830 to

St. Jerome thought it "absurd" that God could be concerned about lowly creatures such as the earthworm . . .

1890. (Future paleontologists will call it Ur-Wormhaven or Proto-Wormhaven and publish massive books on the "enigma of Wormhaven," and even question whether Wormhaven ever existed, except as a myth.)

The ancients were aware of the value of compost and manure, but Oliver's grandfather was the first modern on record to farm with the well being of the earthworm in mind. In brief, he gathered all manure and vegetable waste into a large pit, where clay and moisture were added. Millions of earthworms filled the pit. At the beginning of spring plowing, the compost pit was "almost a solid mass of earthworms."[8] The compost, worms, and egg capsules were applied to the fields on a regular basis, where the earthworm population probably exceeded one million per acre. The result of this farming was great productivity, no crop failures, and a complete use of all organic materials.

The Oriental approach to intensive farming can be studied in F. H. King's *Farmers of Forty Centuries* (1911). King reminds us that Orientals have prized all organic material and would not consider throwing away vegetable scraps which could go back in the soil. The population of China and Korea could not have survived on soil which was used up and blown away after a few years of exploitation.

Sir Albert Howard (1873-1947), a British agricultural expert in India, became the first modern to break with the new scientific approach. He questioned the simplistic approach of using three chemicals to build up soil which is obviously more complex. He also doubted the nutritional value of crops grown in depleted soil. The Hunsa Indians (now famous through the grains offered by Walnut Acres, Penns Creek, Pennsylvania) used all waste material and thrived, while other sub-groups in India suffered from poor nutritional habits. Howard invented the Indore compost heap, named after Indore, India. He discovered that compost built up the soil while protecting plants against insects and disease. His test of soil fertility was one fat earthworm per shovel of dirt. He was dismayed when he found that many modern techniques decimated the earthworm population.

Howard's discoveries in *An Agricultural Testament* converted Jerome Irving Rodale (1898-1971), who was then involved with taxes and dictionaries. To test Howard's conclusion, Rodale bought a farm in 1940 and launched the enterprise which publishes the magazines *Organic Gardening* and *Prevention*, and a multitude of useful books. Organic gardening was considered proof of insanity a few years ago, but the ecology movement has caught up with Howard's dissent and given people reason to consider a divine plan in nature. Rodale Press has provided much of the material which validates the importance of earthworms to gardening.

Several other figures have played an important role in the growing appreciation of the earthworm. George Sheffield Oliver, previously mentioned, read Darwin's book in 1905 and realized how little Darwin understood the agricultural applications. Oliver was a surgeon who found so much success in landscaping that he built his fortune on it. His secret was the inoculation of soil with earthworm egg capsules! During the Depression, as the Dust Bowl devastated the West, Oliver revealed his secret in his book *Our Friend the Earthworm*, 1937. Thomas Barrett contributed a fine book on using the earthworm for agriculture in 1959, *Harnessing the Earthworm*. Oliver and Barrett were both in the earthworm business, so their publishing efforts were a logical extension of their work.

Henry Hopp, an agricultural expert for the U. S. Department of Agriculture, deviated from the "scientific" standard in the late 1940's and published articles arguing for the benefits of earthworm tillage in farming, in fighting erosion, and in ecology. Although slighting references to the noble earthworm can be found in many books in print, Hopp's conclusions are generally accepted. Most of the earthworm classics, including Darwin's, can be obtained through Ronald Gaddie's Bookworm Publishing Company in Ontario, California.

The earthworm is starting to get the attention it deserves, from organic gardeners (Jerry Minnich's *The Earthworm Book*); from vermiculturalists (Ronald Gaddie's *Earthworms for Ecology and Profit*); and from scientists (C. A. Edwards and J. R. Lofty, *Biology of Earthworms*). If the gardener becomes truly interested in the relationships established by the Creator, then the books on worms will lead to ones on spiders, ladybugs, praying mantises, ants, birds, squirrels, molds, weeds, herbs, soil, and more.

Tunneling and Infiltration of Water

I contend that the person who understands the design and purpose of the earthworm will also appreciate the vast potential of the creature for the garden. First of all, the earthworm is a creature of the soil, tunneling through all varieties with the greatest of ease, a talent we take for granted until the benefits of this tunneling becomes more obvious to us. In many ways the earthworm best resembles a tiny hydraulic drill, using its hard, pointed prostomium to probe through soil, its mouth to swallow whatever cannot be pushed aside, its bristles (*cetae*), rings of muscle and intestinal pressure to worm its way through the toughest barriers. A friend noted that earthworms repeatedly burrowed through a layer of fresh asphalt she put around her garage to promote drainage.

Soil itself is not only a creation of God but an ocean of life, filled with trillions of creatures which work together in providing food for one another and for all those who live above the soil. The bottom limit of soil is bedrock, which is so strong that we anchor our skyscrapers and bridges in this base. Above the bedrock may be many feet of soil, caused by the erosion of rocks, which may not be productive. The soil may be mixed with rocks, clay, and gravel. The top layer is the productive soil, especially the upper 12 inches. One can find as much as 20 feet of top soil in some areas or as little as a few inches. Light soil is full of sand and drains well, often too well. Heavy soil is full of fine clay particles which hold water so well that drainage can be a problem. Loamy soil is high in organic content or humus and may lean to the sandy or clay side.

The three major chemicals in soil are nitrogen (N), which promotes leafy growth; phosphorus (P), which helps the flower and fruits; and potassium (K), which is good for the roots. Many other elements are found in soil and contribute to healthy plants, including: iron, calcium, magnesium, manganese, copper, zinc, and boron. Organic material in the soil contributes to its crumb structure. Clay particles exchange mineral ions very easily and thereby add to the soil's fertility.

Lots of animals live in the soil. Actinomycetes are the bacteria which give soil its earthy smell. Protozoa also live in the soil, along with fungi. Springtails, a tiny insect which lives on fungi and organic material, may be the most populous and least known animal in God's Kingdom. Mites, millipedes, centipedes, sowbugs, beetles, and ants also populate the soil, each with his appointed task. We seldom think that we not only disturb an earthworm with each shovel of soil, but an entire metropolis of life which enlivens the basis of all our food.

The burrowing of the earthworm has a number of positive effects on the soil. The first and most obvious benefit is mixing the soil. Darwin has shown that earthworms bring soil up to the surface in the castings. All layers are mixed gradually, though not completely (unless the population of earthworms is very high, under controlled conditions). Many experts pooh-pooh this activity since the amount moved per earthworm per day is quite small, equal to his body weight. Unlike the gardener, the earthworm works continuously, without any tools, being careful to leave plants and delicate roots undisturbed. The loosening effect alone promotes growth in plants, because plants do not grow in soil but between soil particles.

The surest way to eliminate all plant growth is simply to walk on the same soil daily. It will not quickly recover from the damaging effects of compaction, which will make the ground bare of vegetation, unless an organic covering (dead grass, leaves, or manure) is provided to entice the earthworms back to that area. Productive soil is always springy, spongy, full of air and ready to absorb rain. Earthworm tunneling accomplishes it.

Most earthworms work in the top 12 inches of soil, where almost all plants send their roots. Even trees do most of their feeding in the top foot of soil. The thoughtful gardener and orchard owner will covet an army of earthworms carefully loosening the soil around the tender feeder roots of his fruit trees. Although a rototiller can move a huge amount of soil at once, the effort requires expense, labor, fuel, possible soil compaction, and probably damage to valued plants. Rototilling, which has value in certain circumstances, will certainly kill many earthworms while flailing the soil. Faulkner and advocates of mulch farming have questioned whether the visual benefits of turning over vast quantities of soil are worth the price of subsequent soil erosion, compaction, and destruction of soil structure. Certainly the lowly earthworm affirms the conclusion of the Aesop fable of the Tortoise and the Hare: "Slow and steady wins the race."

Tunneling provides a number of other benefits worth considering, all essential to productive soil:

1.   Aeration—introducing small air pockets into the soil. Soil without air is called a bog, noted for bad smells and exotic plants. When the earthworm opens up channels for air to penetrate the soil, healthy bacteria and molds grow, speeding up the constant decaying process which feeds all living things.

2.   Infiltration of water—making little channels for water to enter the soil, as opposed to running over the top and eroding the best topsoil. When water hits dried soil, it tends to run off and take the finest and best soil particles in the stream. If the soil is peppered with worm holes, the rain will percolate down, decreasing erosion.

3.   Humification—taking organic material below the surface. Worms like to bring dead vegetation into their tunnels, a small favor which adds up as ground litter goes beneath the surface to rot or be digested. Soil with a higher content of organic material will hold water better, support more soil creatures, and be more fertile.

4.   Fertilization—adding nutrients to the soil. The worm excretes

nitrogen compounds which do not burn plants, unlike most animal manure. Their casts on the surface and in tunnels add to the fertility and structure of the soil. Their calcium glands make the soil sweeter, which benefits all plants except blueberries, evergreens, and rhododendrons, all of which prefer acid soil.

Feeding

The active earthworm, with his God-given talent for tunneling, also excels in the area of feeding. Not only is the feeding itself valuable, since it removes dead organic material from the surface of the soil, but so also is the final product of feeding, the cast. The earthworm itself is little more than mouth, stomach, and intestine, wrapped in muscular rings. Although the digestive process has proven to be complex and impressive for such a simple creature, we can see that the Lumbricid has little more purpose in life than to tunnel, feed, and reproduce.

Food, which can be soil or organic material (leaves, manure, grass) enters the earthworm through the prostomium at the anterior. In the pharynx, food starts to break down through mixing, moistening, and secretions (amylase, and from the calciferous glands, calcium carbonate). The calciferous glands seem to regulate pH (acid) for the earthworm, which cannot and will not abide in overly acid soil. They neutralize acid for their own benefit (we imagine) and thereby increase soil productivity. The liming effect releases other soil chemicals for plants to use, since an acidic soil binds up those chemicals.

The calciferous glands alone should blow the mental circuits of the most devout evolutionist. It would be enough if the earthworm did so much good from tunneling and fertilizing the soil. But those tiny calcium carbonate factories attached to the worm mean that the worm can create sweet soil for himself while benefiting every plant we use for food. So here we have both a double purpose and a marvelous design by God, before we even ask what drives the worm to tunnel so obsessively and mate so frequently.

The crop of the earthworm stores food until it is ground up in the muscular gizzard. Soil particles and very small bits of stone serve as abrasive material to grind up tough materials. In the process, soil particles and small stones are ground finer than before, as Darwin has pointed out. Fine soil particles are easily lost through water and wind erosion, so they need to be replenished constantly. What other creature, great or small, grinds fresh soil particles for us? Food leaves the gizzard and enters the intestine, which continues the digestive process. The earthworm excretes solid material castings from its anus and nitrogenous liquid through its nephridia. It also secretes mucous, which adds to the nitrogen in the soil.

The end result of earthworm feeding is to make the soil better, for a number of reasons. First of all, the earthworm is a "colloid mill," a small chemical plant which produces an array of chemicals and concentrates other chemicals in its castings, mucous, and nephridia excretions.[9] The colloids give structure to the soil. Secondly, the earthworm increases the bacteria and breaks down humus material in its castings. Finally, it humifies the soil through its pulling down of organic material into the soil for feeding. Earthworms may seem insignificant, only weighing 1/30th of an ounce each, but they are the most abundant, active, and beneficial of the higher soil creatures.

Comparing them to the billions of bacteria in the soil, we see that earthworms accomplish more than the simple bacteria. Bacteria and molds are essential in breaking down plant and animal tissue, but earthworms do more than break down humus material. Ants tunnel, aerate, and even humify the soil to a great degree; they are indeed the hardworking garbage collectors of the insect world, carrying off the corpses of dead insects. Still, earthworms are never harmful pests, as ants often are, and earthworms do not have the disgusting trait of protecting and caring for other pests (as ants do for aphids). Nor do earthworms get into the house, except for when my brother collected a bunch and left them in the basement in a tin can, only to forget them for two weeks, until our mother asked tough questions about a horrible odor downstairs.

Food Preferences

Considering the vast amount of beneficial work done by the earthworm, I decided to find out the best way to encourage their multiplication. Their primary needs are food and water, and they thrive when copious amounts of both are supplied. Earthworms also prefer shade and moderate temperatures. The greatest populations are found in pastures of grass and clover, in fields of legumes, in clay rather than sand (due to minerals and moisture in clay), in soils which are not too acid, in moist rather than dry soil. Earthworms thrive in manured soil, but they are scarce in areas covered densely by leaves or pine needles. Leaves will at first give off chemicals which annoy earthworms, while pine needles

St. Francis preaches to the worms

Late for the sermon again!

create an acidic soil.

Earthworms turn their food into castings (see following section), the only kind of excrement which can be applied to plants without burning them, so it seems reasonable to supply as much food as possible. The ultimate worm food for the garden is compost, which is better than manure in many respects. Compost is the final product of the decay of plant and animal matter, mixed with some soil and manure.

Compost is better because it is pure food. A layer of compost over the garden area will supply the perfect food for earthworms, a blanket of humus to hold in moisture and hold down weeds, and a source of nutrition for plant and worm alike. The section on composting ("Compost Yourself") explains how God has designed a vast army of creatures to reduce organic material into components which can be used again. The earthworm serves as the final agent of reduction, taking the cooled down humus material into its gut and rendering it into castings. Compost provides the highest possible concentration of earthworms per square foot, and the greatest difficulty for a gardener is keeping things from sprouting right out of the heap.

Although most compost is made in a pit or a pile, mulch provides another way of making compost on the spot. No one ever has enough compost, but mulch can be made out of grass clippings, newspapers, leaves, hay, straw, or wood chips. (See "What is Mulch?" p. 52.) Mulch decomposes, creating compost and feeding worms in the process. In fact, worms will attack any organic material left on the surface, with the help of molds, bacteria, millipedes, and other agents of reduction. Mulch also holds in moisture while providing food. Mulch can take nitrogen out of the soil as it rots down, but this has been overplayed in many books. It holds down weeds and keeps plant roots cool and moist. I use spoiled hay, obtained free from a horse breeder, and grass clippings. Under every gob of rotting hay or grass, there is moist soil and a fat earthworm.

Manure is an outstanding soil amendment, but it is difficult to obtain for many people. In most places composted cow manure can be bought in sacks for a reasonable price. Earthworms thrive on manure, the older the better. Raw manure is often too strong for earthworms to attack right away, partly because it gets hot so fast, but obviously a garden with manure added will produce bountifully. The worm gardener will buy or apply manure in the fall (when most things are on sale), the best time to feed the soil and earthworms for the following spring. Since earthworms pull under the food they need, there is no reason to till the manure under the soil.

Many people neglect to feed their soil for free, even while they are paying someone to haul away newspapers, branches, leaves, grass clippings, and garbage. Newspapers serve as a quick rotting mulch, especially good under grass clippings or other more natural cover. Branches and twigs can be broken up and used in the soil, or piled up to be used by birds for cover. (Birds love brush piles and branches laid on the ground. The branches help them look for insects and worms without giving themselves away. Earthworms are very sensitive to vibration.) Leaves and grass clippings make excellent mulch; grass during the summer, leaves for the winter. A thick layer of leaves will prevent the soil from freezing quickly, allowing the earthworms to feed and tunnel all winter long, though at a slower pace. The leaves will not be so concentrated that they would stifle worm growth, as they might in a mature forest.

Garbage can be dug into the soil or used in composting. Meat attracts carnivores and rodents, so meat scraps are hauled away. Like many organic gardeners, we haul grass, leaves, and other materials to our house. In Midland, the utility company delivered a truck of woodchips for free.

Earthworms are mostly moisture and need plenty of it to survive and thrive. They do not drown in water, even though many worms are found on the sidewalks after a heavy storm (for reasons unknown). Egg casings (also called cocoons) can survive extremes of dryness and cold, but earthworms cannot. Watering the garden and lawn will not only benefit the plants but even more so the worms. The plants and grass need the earthworms as much as they need the water, for the continuous action of the earthworm provides loose aerated soil and a steady supply of castings.

Castings

In order to appreciate the value of earthworm casts, we should first imagine Thomas Barrett's one-ton earthworm. Barrett postulates his theoretical monster on the basis of an earthworm population of one million per acre, which can be matched and exceeded. Combining the million earthworms into one creature would give us a one-ton beast which is over six miles long. Now the earthworm seems more noteworthy. On one acre he will move one ton of soil a day and deposit one ton of castings a day. Adjusting for the one quarter acre land a typical yard occupies, that would equal 12 and 1/2 bags of composted cow manure (40 pounds each) every day, at a cost of approximately $25, just to match the increased fertility of the soil. Most of us are not up to moving 500 pounds of soil each day, week after week, in addition to the purchase and application of manure.

Clearly the earthworm can directly affect the fertility of the soil. Some may counter that the earthworm merely redistributes what was already present in the soil; but that does not account for the food manufactured by plants in a natural setting, nor does it account for the necessary changes in any form of soil improvement from the raw state to the form in which the nutrition is available to plants. Nothing will grow in a bag of N-P-K fertilizer. In fact, a spill will burn out any plant life at ground zero, just as most fresh manure will. The earthworm not only reduces a tremendous variety of materials to a fine and non-burning fertilizer, it also tirelessly places the castings exactly where they are needed, in the root zone. Above ground castings may bother the people who adore a perfect lawn or golf green, but those are separate religions.

The composition of castings is quite interesting. Partly they are made of finely ground soil particles. In addition, they have a cohesiveness which binds them together and adds to the water stability of the soil. In other words, they do not break down quickly and dissolve in water. This reduces soil erosion by forming soil aggregates - crumb structure.

Plants require nutrition to thrive, and casts provide basic elements for growth. After observing a farm which used manure regularly, Sir Albert Howard noted, in the preface to Darwin's earthworm book.

> Here earthworms were abundant and in some of the old tunnels I frequently observed the reaction of the roots of the potato (King Edward) to fresh worm casts. The fine roots often followed these tunnels downwards, but whenever they passed the earthworm casts a fine network of roots was given off laterally which penetrated the casts in all directions.[10]

Worm casts are not the same as manufactured fertilizer sold in a bag. Like animal manure, it does not have a concentration of nitrogen, phosphorous, and potassium, but the three macronutrients are present as .5-2.0 percent nitrogen, .06-.68 percent phosphorous, and .10-.68 percent potassium. Although this is modest in comparison with inorganic fertilizer, a comparison of casts to ordinary soil is illuminating. Casts are 500 percent richer in nitrogen, 700 percent richer in available phosphates, and 1100 percent richer in potassium than soil.[11] Although earthworms will not thrive in a soil too acid, their castings make the soil more alkaline or "sweet" with 150 percent more calcium than the surrounding soil.[12]

Earthworm castings also increase the number of bacteria present in the soil. Gaddie reports that casts contain 300-500 percent the number of bacteria as the surrounding soil. The deep digging nightcrawler has about the same number of bacteria, while the shallow digging and humus loving red wiggler has 1000 percent more bacteria.[13]

The role of bacteria is quite complex, but it seems that a high proportion of bacteria is a measure of productive soil. Secondly, bacteria and molds battled against each other (example: the mold penicillin versus the streptococcus bacterium) in the soil long before they waged war in our bodies. A high level of organic materials will work together to balance the disease causing organisms with the beneficial ones. When man does not interfere with and wipe out the predators along with the prey, the harmful forms of life are kept under control in the garden and soil. Edwards and Lofty have shown that earthworms have an adverse affect on apple scab disease, partially because they pull the leaves underground, where the spores cannot spread.[14]

Death - the Ultimate Sacrifice

As remarkable as the earthworm's contributions may be to the soil, through its tunneling, mixing, humifying and fertilizing, a final beneficial effect is realized when the earthworm dies. The earthworm's dry weight is 72 percent protein, muscle made up of nitrogen, so its death means a substantial contribution to the nitrogen enrichment of the soil. According to Lawrence and Millar, 70 percent of the nitrogen in worm tissue is available to plants two weeks after the creature's death. Using Barrett's one ton earthworm concept, that would mean ten pounds of ammonium and 19 pounds of nitrate.[15] The earthworms die throughout the year, but the greatest amount of loss would occur in the dry months of July and August, providing an additional boost to the parched plants. The advantage of this form of fertilization is that the slow decay offers a gradual supply of nutrients in an available form.

Earthworms may not die in a dry spell but go into a state of diapause,

Worms & Shakespeare

42

emptying their digestive organs, rolling up in ball, and waiting for better times. This would also add to the soil's fertility.

Reproduction

Each earthworm contains both male and female sex organs, but they do not fertilize themselves in most cases. Earthworms look for other earthworms of the same species, nightcrawlers above ground, and other species below ground. Earthworms cannot be hybridized because of size differences. A close match is needed for the male gonads to fertilize the female gonads of the other worm. Therefore we will never see a night crawler mated with a red wiggler to create giant red wigglers.

When earthworms mate, a cocoon or egg case forms on the clitellum. The worm is able to slide the cocoon off its body once it becomes hard. Each casing contains one or two baby earthworms (except for manure worms, which have up to 20). The cocoons will hatch in two or three weeks, if weather permits and moisture is adequate. Egg cases will survive when earthworms would die; thus, the supply is replenished in the damp weather of spring and fall each year. George S. Oliver used egg cases to transform his garden and the gardens of many clients. The advantage of egg cases is that the hatched worms are not so prone to die, as commercially bred, spoiled earthworms may.

A British minister once noted that earthworms: "are much addicted to venery," so we can count on them to increase and multiply, especially the ones which are industrious soil improvers: red wigglers, nightcrawlers, and field worms.[16] There is still a debate about whether one can introduce a beneficial species of earthworm into the garden. A ton of earthworms added to poor soil will result in one ton of dead earthworms. Good soil will already have a plentiful supply of active earthworms. Nevertheless, one can work on both sides of the equation (active earthworms = productive soil) at the same time.

The ideal breeding ground for earthworms is compost or mulch, because both provide food, darkness, and moisture, plus protection from sudden temperature changes. When compost is made in a pit, earthworms will invade at the proper time and multiply by the thousands. The distribution of compost will result in the scattering of earthworms and their cocoons among globs of their favorite health food. (I do not suggest tilling compost under but just the opposite. Compost belongs on the top of the soil, to serve as a weed barrier, a food supply for earthworms, a moist mulch covering for plants and worms alike, a humus blanket to be converted into worm castings placed where plants need them most, a reason for earthworms to tunnel tirelessly in the soil.) Mulch will accomplish the same results, although it will take longer to break down into the soil. However, one can obtain a truck of mulch easier than a truck of compost. (See "Compost Yourself" and "What is Mulch?")

The study of earthworm reproduction leads to obvious conclusions. If earthworms improve soil at a rate directly related to their numbers, then we must do everything possible to encourage their venery. When the temperature is too cold, "Earthworms retreat to their burrows, coil themselves in tight balls to conserve moisture, and think not of sex at all."[17] Mulch can offer earthworms protection from sudden temperature drops which repress the romantic urge and literally freeze their tails off. Mulch will allow reproduction, tunneling, and feeding to continue longer into the winter and to start sooner in the spring.

In the summer, lack of moisture is a greater problem. Then mulch will conserve moisture and provide cool shade for the natural urges of the lubricids. Sprinkling the garden and lawn during the dry days will also help considerably. Some people store rain water, conserving water while offering the plants their favorite drink, free from chlorine.

In addition, one may purchase red wigglers to introduce into the compost, mulch, and garden. I bought 1,000 red wigglers for $9 from Jimmie Carter's cousin in Georgia. They came in a small paper bag—very small. I put piles of them in the two main gardens and the large compost pit early in the fall. Days later, they were spreading out into the area around the inoculation point. They flourished later under the rabbit cages, in plastic swimming pools filled with soil. The nitrogen cycle was complete. We fed the rabbits from the garden. They gave nitrogen rich food to the earthworms below. The earthworms multiplied and made castings for the garden, which fed the rabbits.

Earthworm Observations

Earthworms are amazingly hardy, more than we could hope for, if we tried to design a creature which plowed and fertilized at the same time. One example: we used to feed birds and squirrels on our concrete patio the year around. An elm tree stump was placed on the concrete to provide a perch for the birds and squirrels. When I lifted the stump to move it, I noticed that five earthworms of various sizes were happily living between concrete and rotting wood. The wood offered moisture, food, and shade for the worms, but I do not know how they got there. There are many anecdotes in the earthworm community about lumbricids showing up in soils where they had been apparently absent, as soon as water and humus were provided.

Although earthworms are hardy and prolific, they also have a suicidal bent. The nightcrawler habit of pulling leaves into the entrance of their tunnels draws attention to their hideouts. Other worms wiggle around near the top of the soil, enabling the robin to pounce on them and make a quick meal. A mature compost pit teems with earthworms, who hate sunlight. When shade falls on the compost pit, robins will hop around, pulling up dozens of worms. We called one robin Porky because he never bothered to fly away to safety when we approached. He just waddled under the bushes and waited for us to walk way. When we dug into his compost we found an earthworm in every handful of leaves, which were quite old by then.

Earthworms are fond of mulch, especially the easily composted types, which are high in nitrogen: grass, clover, weeds, hay. Some people claim that a mulch will shed rain or absorb so much moisture that nothing reaches the soil. This seems highly unlikely and not supported by my experience. A light rain or watering will not penetrate the mulch, but it will aid in the decomposition of the material. Except during a severe drought, soil is never dried out under a mulch, which releases water during decomposition. Because of the increased tunneling of the earthworm population, the soil under mulch will not become waterlogged as easily.

I put huge amounts of organic material on top of the soil in the Wormhaven.1 garden: 20 bales of moldy hay, a truckload of cedar bark and needles from the utility company, 60 bags of leaves, and all the grass clippings from two yards. All of it disappeared from the work of soil creatures and birds gathering nesting material. When I put newspapers under a layer of grass mulch to keep the weeds down in the corn, I found earthworms literally devouring the news. They enjoyed the front pages, sports section, even the society page and want ads. I count each pound of organic material a pound of future earthworm castings. What others hauled to the curb, I retrieved for the garden.

TWO

Gardening for the Benefit of Earthworms

"ꓭ ehold this compost! behold it well!
Perhaps every mite has once form'd part of a sick person—yet
behold!
The grass of spring covers the prairies,
The bean bursts noiseless through the mould in the garden,
The delicate spear of the onion pierces upward...
Now I am terrified at the Earth, it is that calm and patient,
It grows such sweet things out of such corruptions...."
                    Walt Whitman, *Leaves of Grass*, "This Compost"

Starting the Garden

Some people may have had bad experiences with gardening because
they started wrong. The temptation is to begin in the spring, but that is
six months too late, missing at least one (if not two periods of intense,
beneficial earthworm activity—fall and early spring.) When gardeners
turn over the lawn for the first time in the spring and try to add organic
material too quickly, they can use up available nitrogen in the soil.[18]

An old garden does not need to be plowed up after the produce is gone
in the fall. The annual plants may be left to rot, their roots holding the
soil in place while slowly decaying. Decomposition will feed the soil
creatures. Permanent plants, such as roses and raspberries, can have
their mulch renewed in the fall. I use grass clippings and leaves. Excess

leaves are put in a compost bin for use in the spring, not bagged and hauled away.

If a new garden is anticipated for the spring, then the sod should be dug up or rototilled. Sometimes it is easier to compost the sod in another area by itself, because sod strips weigh down a compost heap and make it difficult to turn. When sod is piled upside down, it reduces down rather quickly, thanks to the rich topsoil, the nitrogen in the grass, and the soil creatures which stowaway on the strips. I created a small pit for sod strips, which later became the site for parsley and asparagus. The soil was always jello-like from that time on, quivering when I stepped on it.

The soil of the Great Plains used to quiver when people jumped out of their wagons. Centuries of prairie grass composted by earthworms filled the earth with the gelatinous quality of humus and the productive power of organic soil. One scientist wrote: "A man jumping off a haywagon onto virgin prairie sod may see the tremor of the impact for several feet around, and you easily notice this soft resilience while you walk across native prairie."[19]

An agriculture expert from Dow Chemical said that it was difficult to deplete the nitrogen in Illinois topsoil when they wanted to do an experiment. They had to grow corn in the same plot of land three years in a row to get the soil nitrogen low enough. He slapped his leg, exclaiming, "Three years!" laughing about soil so rich that corn could not rob it fast enough for Dow. Could it be God's design and purpose to have His rolling prairies turned into amber waves of grain, to feed the world?

One of life's great mysteries (for the rationalist) is the absence of trees in the Great Plains. Forests should have "evolved" in the soil, but did not, allowing the earthworm to transform the prairie grass into 30 feet of topsoil. One naturalist wrote: "Many men have wondered about prairie, are still wondering about prairie and the forces that created and maintained it. As far back as 1870, a midwestern scientist observed that the treelessness of prairie was 'one of the most hackneyed questions' in natural history."[20]

> To make a prairie it takes a clover
> and one bee, —
> One clover, and a bee,
> And revery.
> The revery alone will do
> If bees are few.
>   Emily Dickinson

Starting in September or October, the garden area can receive grass clippings, leafy kitchen scraps, and ground up leaves. The leaves can be piled up on or near the garden and mowed with the lawnmower. Shredding leaves will make them rot into the soil faster by increasing the surface area and making the surface vulnerable to mold. Several inches of organic material can be piled onto the garden and held in place with some heavy tree branches. Birds will perch on the branches and make use of dead air spaces when they need shelter. Insects will try to survive the winter in a pile of branches, providing food for the birds.

Fall is a good time to apply manure. Most garden centers are trying to get rid of bagged, composted manure at this time. Earthworms love manure, so manure applications cannot be overdone. If the gardener has good things to say about horses, cows, and rabbits at social gatherings, he will soon find out who raises these animals and wants to reduce the size of their piles.

When our son Martin was nine years old, he energetically helped us pitch manure into a friend's pickup truck. Horse apples were flying in every direction until we slowed him down. The truck owner mentioned how he pitched a whole load in without closing the cab window. The front seat was well fertilized. After some aerobic manure tossing we took the load to the Midland parsonage and more to the truck owner's garden. We gave our neighbor three wheelbarrow loads of manure, which they regarded as the greatest possible gift. In return, they snowplowed our long sidewalk all winter without being asked. The stewardship of God's Creation draws people together.

For the advanced gardener, fall is the time to apply compost. For those who hurry their compost, spreading it out will give it the air needed to finish up during the winter. Spreading compost will not only feed worms already present but also add new worms and egg cases to the garden area. By emptying the compost pit or bin in the fall, room is created in the bins for the winter compost. The amount of organic material for composting during winter is remarkable. By spring, the bin can be filled all over again with weeds, kitchen scraps, some manure, extra leaves, and other materials. The organic material should be user-friendly: damp, easily rotted, and high in humus. A log will rot very slowly because of its low level of nitrogen and solid structure. Twigs will compost faster, especially if they are broken, crushed, or mowed. Green leafy matter has a high content of moisture and nitrogen, so it will heat up and reduce fast.

Some examples will show how easy and fun this can be. On the clay soil on the south side of our house in Midland, I put a fall mulch of ground sycamore leaves mixed with horse manure. Sycamore leaves are just like leather, so they must be torn up to rot. In the early spring more sycamore leaves had blown into the mulch, so everything was raked out and mowed again. By June the mulch was gone. The clay soil was powdery, friable, and riddled with worm holes. It also looked fluffed up, like bread dough which had risen.

On another piece of land, I put three wheelbarrow loads of manure onto an area 2' by 5', then covered the manure with loads of fall leaves. These disappeared by spring, with only a trace remaining. Needless to

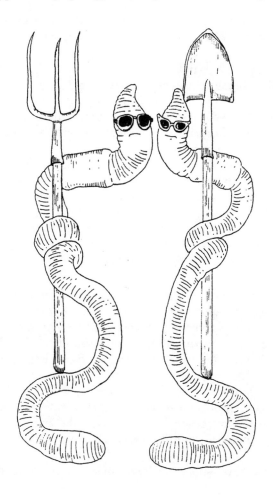

say, the new garden was extremely productive that summer.

The main garden got the complete Wormhaven treatment in the fall of 1982: compost, manure, and ground up leaves. The previous year all the maple leaves had been raked onto the garden with the intention of bagging them up. Good intentions failed and the soggy mess remained until June of 1982, when it was bagged and removed (due to my ignorance). The garden outperformed others, leading me to investigate the reasons. The soft, fertile soil confirmed Ruth Stout's claims for mulch (*How To Have a Green Thumb Without an Aching Back*). Additional reading showed me how the earthworm turned fall mulch into summer fertility.

In 1983, armed with my new shovel (a birthday present from Chris, my understanding wife), I turned over some soil in the main garden, to mix the clay subsoil with top soil. Ambition slackened with rising temperatures, and the remaining garden did not get additional shoveling, or what gardeners call a perspiration mulch. Instead, a thin film of leaves remained. This proved to be such an effective anti-weed mulch (in contrast to the turned soil) that I vowed to let sleeping mulches lie.

Therefore, in the spring, the mulch can remain. It can simply be moved aside for seeds or transplants. It will always be easy to work soil which has been covered all winter with a mulch. Local climate may make slugs a problem, but other causes should be investigated, such as the overcrowding of vine plants (an ideal slug climate). Mulchers and non-mulchers will also have slug problems at the same time, due to weather, leading me to believe that mulch itself is not the key variable.

Fall Cover Crops

Faulkner's *Plowman's Folly* was one of the first books to show the value of cover crops and to question the effectiveness of the moldboard plow. The purpose of cover crops becomes more obvious when we look at God's Creation. When an area is laid bare by bulldozers, the first growth we see in the raw, eroded, rocky soil is that of weeds. Ragweeds and other hardy, successful plants will send down long, tough roots. The weeds grow well in poor soil and produce humus, which feeds a growing earthworm population, which in turn creates a new layer of topsoil. As the soil becomes richer, other plants take over. Insect, bird, and mammal life will occupy the once bare soil. In time, a hardwood forest will normally develop.

The cover crop is a substitute for the first invasion of weeds, although there is no reason why weeds cannot be used. Some would object to the increase of weed seeds in the top layer of soil, but a dedicated mulcher can take care of that. Cover crops are grown and then tilled into the soil, so that their roots and above ground vegetation will rot and feed the soil. Worm fanciers realize that the cover crop feeds the soil population, which God has provided to turn raw organic material into a growing medium.

Joseph Cocannouer wrote a revolutionary book, *Weeds—Guardians of the Soil*, 1950, showing that God has a purpose in His use of weeds. They can be companion plants in the garden. They can trap insects, renew soil, and pump nutrients from the subsoil. Many people despise certain plants as weeds simply because those plants are so successful. The dandelion was brought to America as a herb. Its leaves are very nutritious and good in salads. Its flowers can be made into wine because of their sugar content. Its root can be turned into a coffee substitute. If a dandelion needed a lot of help to survive, people would plant it in their lawns for the bright yellow flower and the parachuting puffball of seeds. But they curse the dandelion for having those qualities which the seed catalogues praise when selling their newest cultivars: "This plant will survive drought, pests, neglect, heavy traffic, and still provide a summer of cheery butter-gold flowers which will turn into enchanting seed heads of air launched messengers of joy." When I pull dandelions from the lawn, I often find an earthworm curled around the taproot.

Few people want to plant weeds as cover crops, so they use a legume (bean family), clover, or alfalfa—all known for fixing nitrogen in the soil. This fixing process takes place in nodules on the roots, where bacteria turn gaseous nitrogen into solid nitrogen compounds usable by plants. Nitrogen is abundant in the atmosphere but often sparse in soil, especially when heavy feeders have grown there (corn, grass, pumpkins, cabbage). A cover crop is tilled into the soil or left to rot into the earth.

Farmers use alfalfa as a nitrogen machine and food for the cattle, but gardeners may want to use clover. Clover is second only to alfalfa in producing nitrogen. White clover has the triple advantage of self-seeding, spreading through its root system, and fixing nitrogen in the soil. Clover, like rye, has a tremendous root system. Live roots prevent soil erosion. Dead roots feed the soil creatures. Bees love the blossoms, and so do rabbits. Our stand of white clover at Wormhaven.1 may have kept the garden from damage from wild rabbits. I like the blossoms and the work they do for the soil. I did not want to pay a lawn chemical company to kill the nitrogen fixing clover so they could spray nitrogen compounds on the grass.

Children taught me to pick blossoms and give them a sniff. They smell just like bubble gum. Enjoying the sweet breeze which blows across a field of clover is one of the great pleasures God gives to us.

Rye is also used as a fall cover crop, because of its huge root system. Each plant will produce miles of roots, which penetrate and loosen heavy soil. Annual rye will sprout and grow, but die during the winter, feeding earthworms and giving them a blanket for the cold weather. Cover crops work so well that they are often called "green manure." It is much easier to sprinkle a pound of seed in the fall than to shovel a truckload of manure, and yet the seed will grow enough to equal a load of manure. God, plants, and soil creatures make gardening easy.

What Is Mulch?

Mulch for the Wormhaven garden includes any material that has lived: leaves, grass, newspaper, leafy kitchen garbage, banana peels, pulled up weeds, hay, stray, garden plants past their prime, sawdust, twigs, and so forth. People use plastic film and aluminum foil, but those materials cost money and contribute nothing to the life, liberty, and pursuit of happiness of the earthworm. Rocks and woodchips can be used, but they are considered a permanent mulch, not readily composted.

In fact, all mulch can be properly considered compost in the making. God has been composting since the Creation, with excellent results. Leaves—which we carefully rake, bag, and pay money to remove, provide the ideal mulch for the plant which drops them. Oak trees need the acid soil created by oak leaves. The prairie of the Midwest has the richest topsoil in the nation, simply because the dense root systems and decayed grasses have been converted by earthworms and micro-organisms into the perfect medium for grass. Many people rake up or catch their grass clippings, pay to have them removed, then pay to have their nitrogen replaced by a truck!

Everything gets mulched in the Wormhaven garden, with excellent results. One way to effect mulching is to use wide rows of plants, an 18 inch row of beans rather than a single row. Or pumpkins may be planted in the corn patch. Thick plantings or companion plantings will shade the soil, preserve moisture, and prevent weeds from forming. Plants like to keep their feet cool and moist. The more a plant demands water and nutrition (as do corn, pumpkins, roses), the more a mulch will help growth.

Mulching with organic materials means using waste materials for

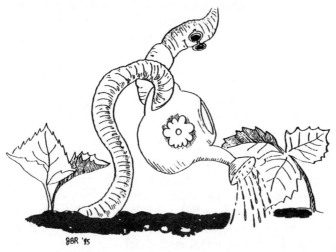

BBR '95

the benefit of the garden. One of the best is grass from the lawn. No matter what other books say, I think grass can be used fresh and green, or old and slimy from the garbage bag. I tossed hot, steamy, smelly grass clippings from the garbage bag onto the green peppers and saw the mess turn into a light, fine mulch, without damaging the plants. The green peppers thrived. Earthworms love grass, reaching their greatest numbers in grassland meadows. Therefore, they will pull down the dead grass of the mulch as they multiply, according to God's plan. Mulch can be pushed up against the plant without hurting it. A few weeds may poke through, but they can be pulled out and added to the mulch. (Let the punishment fit the crime.)

Another good source of mulch comes from trees. Fresh leaves are chemically programmed by God to kill competition, so they inhibit growth at first. Fortunately, most leaves drop when the garden is dormant. They can be ground up by the lawnmower and then dampened to encourage rot. In early spring they can be ground up again, if necessary. Nothing needs to be raked up in the spring. Most weeds will be inhibited by a thin layer of leaves. Earthworms will multiply under leaves and turn them into castings. Leaves hold water better than most media and they contain a wealth of minerals from the subsoil, where trees obtain their water. Even the leaves in the gutter should be returned to garden, to renew the soil.

Woodchips, often obtained from the street department or utility company, can be used as a semi-permanent mulch. The larger the individual chips, the slower they will break down. If an area is well

53

established with a certain plant, woodchips will keep down the weeds, hold moisture, and slowly feed the soil. Woodchips can also be used to smother a heavily weeded area. A few wheelbarrows of cedar mulch turned a weed patch behind our garage into an attractive area dominated by some cabbage, cauliflower, and cannas. Our neighbor's child said, "Your yard smells like Christmas!" Later I stuck a shovel into the mulch and found an earthworm lodged in the woodchips, happily enjoying the moisture, darkness and food. Only its tail remained rooted in the soil beneath.

Rocks seem to be wrong for mulch, but they can be used effectively. One surprising result of my laziness, when I failed to remove all the limestone gravel from where I planted peas, was a rich harvest of delicious peas for 3-4 weeks. Later I learned that peas cannot abide acid soil and are shallow rooted. Therefore the lime leaching from the gravel sweetened the soil without impairing the growth of the peas. Beans did less well in the same spot, but cherry tomatoes flourished.

Compost Yourself

Compost can be considered the most important contribution one makes to the garden, more important than manure or fertilizer.[21] Compost is the end product of a decomposing pile or pit of organic matter, primarily leafy material, manure, and soil. Compost promotes and transports earthworms. Compost is not new. For centuries it has been known that old or composted manure helps crops more than fresh manure, which can burn plants. Sir Albert Howard invented the modern compost pile when he sought to improve agricultural methods in India. Initially it served to stretch out the supply of manure, which was used up quickly in the heat of India. Since then, compost has grown to be the essential ingredient of every productive garden.

Mulch and compost are not entirely different. Mulch is applied on top of the soil and decomposes, feeding the earthworms while holding in moisture. Compost is often applied as mulch but is also mixed with soil. Compost is essentially a finished product while mulch is always being reduced by the creatures God designed to reduce organic matter to the building blocks of life.

The two compost bins at the New Ulm parsonage bear silent witness in a special way to the power of God's Creation, in a special way, since God uncreates as impressively as He creates. Uncreates? Imagine a Ford auto plant where old cars are brought back and reduced not to scrap but to all the original elements from which they were made—with no toxins or harmful residues remaining.

"That would cost trillions of dollars!" But God does it for free in His Creation through a very complicated and superbly organized system which we call composting. Disease is eliminated. No toxins are left. The final product is so productive that gardeners attribute magical qualities to it.

Compost can be made in a pit dug into the ground, in a wooden bin, in piles, or enclosed in wire. The easiest method of making a bin is to circle 10 feet of wire fence, attach it to a post or bush, and fill it. A pit is hard work to dig to a depth of 4 feet. I once got neighborhood boys to name their price for the digging, which they loved. They demanded cash and whatever they could eat at Baskin Robbins Ice Cream. We were all happy at the end of the day. Above ground compost is easier to observe and aerate, but a pit can be turned immediately into a garden of incredible fertility.

Compost should be in the shade, since God made the soil creatures photophobic. They should get enough moisture to stay as damp as a wet rag. The process will speed up with the introduction of air by turning the material, which can be very difficult. An alternative to turning the compost is using sunflower stalks, which rot and create air spaces, or PVC pipes with holes in them. The compost bin should have soil on the bottom, to allow soil creatures to invade.

The recipe for compost is simple: anything which has lived + soil + moisture. Anything which has lived includes: weeds, grass clippings, vegetables and table scraps, leaves, manure, sawdust, peat, spoiled fruit, corn cobs, leather, newspapers, branches, feathers, hair. Meat can be used, but only if gardeners want to attract dogs, cats, and rodents. The organic matter should have a moderate nitrogen content overall, to speed up heating and the reduction process. Dry leaves will compost slowly, unless combined with grass clippings, rabbit or chicken manure. Sawdust and wood will absorb nitrogen at first but release it later. Each ingredient has good and bad qualities. When a wealthy suburb of St. Louis tried to compost huge piles of grass, they got a ferocious ammonia smell from the nitrogen compounds being produced. Soil in the mixture introduces micro-organisms and suppresses odor at the same time. Properly done, a compost site will not be unsightly or smelly.

Several people, including a professor at Wisconsin Lutheran Seminary, have pointed to a trash heap and asked why it was not composting properly. I usually suggest these steps:

1. Build up enough organic mass to get the compost going, three feet high and several feet around.

2. Combine green leafy material with other organic ingredients and soil, to give the nitrogen loving bacteria a chance to heat up the pile.

3. Keep it in the shade, not sunlight, and make sure it is moist all the time. The top may be shaped into a dish, to catch rain, rather than slanted to shed rain.

When we consider how poorly organized we are, even when we are trying to get things done, it is a marvel to see what happens when a compost pile is properly assembled and moistened.

Compost Process

God has assigned mold (fungus) to be the most forceful method of softening dead tissue. Bacteria alone could not rot dead material fast enough, but filaments of mold cover and penetrate dead plant tissue. In compost, damp green grass clippings grow a quick covering of white mold. Molds cannot tolerate high temperatures, which will soon build up in the compost, but they soften plants and serve as food for soil creatures.

A few days after the compost is started, heat-loving bacteria heat up the pile to 170 degrees. They need plenty of nitrogen to do their work, but too much will let the nitrogen escape as gas (that pungent ammonia smell). I built one pit with grass and bunny manure, both high in nitrogen. When I pulled the top layer away, steam came out—on a hot, summer day!

The heat of a good compost pile will kill weed seeds, plant pathogens, and insect larvae. The nitrogen bound up in the plants and manure will be released as ammonia, nitrates, and nitrites. The high heat period will last only a few days, unless the pile is turned over. The heating will be accompanied by a rapid shrinking of the pile.

Low heat bacteria continue the rotting process in the second phase, which begins soon after the heating up. Protozoas and rotifers consume and are consumed. Springtails invade by the millions. The tiny springtails work on nematodes, fungi, arthropod droppings, and rotting vegetation. Mites live on similar fare, but will eat each other as well as insect larvae. Sowbugs, pillbugs, pseudo-scorpions, slugs, and millipedes join the convocation—at the dinner table and on the dinner table. Centipedes clean up the mess, capturing the lower level creatures in their powerful claws, poisoning their prey with homemade toxin.

This process always works the same way. Called by some unknown

If government scientists designed the earthworm . . . .

signal, all the right creatures convene and do their job at exactly the right time. We can see God's design and purpose in compost because the final product is not useless and chaotic but extremely beneficial for the paragon of Creation, man.

The final stage of compost is signaled by the arrival of the king of all soil creatures, the earthworm. He would melt in the initial heating up of the compost and suffer from the early stages of decomposition . . . but he is in his glory when he can invade the compost and make it even better, turning the reduced organic material left into casts, laying cocoons with abandon, lost in a riot of love, leisure, and gourmet eating. But he is not invulnerable, however. The centipedes make sport of him and have him for dinner. The robins will snatch him from his meal and serve him to their baby chicks. The mole will tunnel over and enter the compost for a protein rich supper of earthworms and grubs.

The gardener can sleep at night, knowing God's Creation is at work serving him in the intricate choreography of the compost pile. We can imagine the whole Creation praising God while doing His work according to His Word, and we ought to join them.

Psalm 148

{1} Praise ye the LORD. Praise ye the LORD from the heavens: praise him in the heights.

{2} Praise ye him, all his angels: praise ye him, all his hosts.

{3} Praise ye him, sun and moon: praise him, all ye stars of light.

{4} Praise him, ye heavens of heavens, and ye waters that be above the heavens.

{5} Let them praise the name of the LORD: for he commanded, and they were created.

{6} He hath also stablished them for ever and ever: he hath made a decree which shall not pass.

{7} Praise the LORD from the earth, ye dragons, and all deeps:

{8} Fire, and hail; snow, and vapours; stormy wind fulfilling his word:

{9} Mountains, and all hills; fruitful trees, and all cedars:

{10} Beasts, and all cattle; creeping things, and flying fowl:

{11} Kings of the earth, and all people; princes, and all judges of the earth:

{12} Both young men, and maidens; old men, and children:

{13} Let them praise the name of the LORD: for his name alone is excellent; his glory is above the earth and heaven.

{14} He also exalteth the horn of his people, the praise of all his saints; even of the children of Israel, a people near unto him. Praise ye the LORD.

For the sake of argument, and to protect the "good name" of Charles Darwin, let us picture for a moment every single living organism evolving from random events in the absence of the Creator. How exactly would all those organisms, from the springtail to the robin, know how to work together so well? Aha! It is instinct. Innate cunning. Who imprinted on those arthropodic minds the elaborate liturgy of the compost pile?

In the beginning was the Word, and the Word was with God, and the Word was God. {2} The same was in the beginning with God. {3} All things were made by Him; and without Him was not any thing made that was made. (John 1:1-3)

The believer can see that nothing happens by pure, random chance. If this is so in the soil, how much is it true for those who were not only created by the Word of God, but also redeemed by His suffering on the cross?

If people are not impressed by the composting process, they are still staggered by the results. A compost pile has a way of proving itself, when

a tomato climbs out of the tangle and makes the best plant of the garden, or when a nearby tree or bush suddenly becomes healthy again.

Many people turn old compost pits into gardens. I did this with astonishing results. I emptied the remainder of the winter pit, which was six feet long, four feet across, and four feet deep. Then I dropped some logs in the bottom, along with our Christmas tree, brush, garbage, and weeds. Grass was added before the top layer of compost was put on. I planted sweet white corn, Silver Queen in that area and on some freshly turned sod. On the new ground the corn reached three feet, while the same seed produced eight foot corn a few feet away. Later I mulched the corn on the new ground with grass clippings, newspapers, compost, and manure, and it came close to catching up. The corn plot was planted with Kentucky Wonder pole beans, which climbed the corn, and Atlantic Giant pumpkins, which filled in the rows. The plot also volunteered tomatoes, gourds, and a few weeds, all of enormous vitality.

Many people complain about their clay soil, even though clay is extremely fertile. The fine particles have a very high rate of ion exchange and hold a lot of water. Clay itself is messy to work with and difficult to clean off of root vegetables. I recruited earthworms to change the clay in the Midland yard. I put the first batch of compost on the clay area beneath the pine trees on the northeast corner of our yard. I put on a layer about three inches deep. The soil could hardly be penetrated by a sharp shovel in the dry season. Once a month I tried digging in the pine area. My shovel went through soft compost and then stopped at the clay. After 5 months the shovel went into the clay a foot, the soil soft as butter. I thought, "This is too easy. I'll bet the untreated soil is also soft." I stabbed the shovel into the clay without compost. It would not go in. In contrast, the soil and compost had been mixed thoroughly, was alive with earthworms, and remained soft and friable, easily penetrated by water. No tilling was necessary. The earthworms did their work. Mulch and green manure crops can do the same thing to clay as compost can, but work more slowly.

Sandy soil benefits from compost by becoming a sponge for water instead of a drainpipe for rain. Humus will hold twice its weight in water, so compost added to sandy soil will allow the water to stay in the root zone and feed the plants. Compost will also give the sandy soil more structure.

Questions and Answers about Compost

1. Q. What if I put unfinished compost on the garden?
   A. The compost will finish decomposing in the garden without any problems. It may be harder to handle. Sod can take forever to finish. Half-composted, the clumps look like black sponges, because the roots form a tight mesh.

2. Q. Does compost smell bad?
   A. It can, but it does not have to. Too much food in the compost will make it smell just like old garbage. Too much grass at once can give off ammonia smells. Soil absorbs odor, so I put in layers of soil and put another inch or so on the top of the pile.

3. Q. I hear bad things about grass, weeds, and other compost items. Are they true?
   A. Some people find that grass clippings mat up or believe that leaves should have their own pile. Someone who uses a lot of organic material will find exotic weeds growing here and there. Moldy hay brings in a lot of field weeds, for instance. Some garden plants will multiply through the compost, if the seeds are not killed. It is fun to see them volunteer in strange places. Old gourds erupted out of one compost pit like Jack's beanstalk and covered all the chickenwire on the garage. We enjoyed the harvest of gourds. If weeds come from the compost, we return them to the compost.

4. Q. Do compost bins attract pests?
   A. I have heard of it happening, but I have not seen anything larger than a worm around mine, except for robins and jays. Dogs went after the meat I put in one compost pit, so I stopped using meat. The first compost pile I saw and smelled was simply an open garbage pile, infested with flies, heated by sunshine, a beacon to every pest alive. We were told to run toward the "compost," hold our breath, and toss the

garbage in. I would define that as a health menace,
not a compost bin.

5. Q. Do I need to till compost into the soil?
   A. Only if you just got a rototiller for your birthday.
   Earthworms will till the compost for you. Leave it on
   top of the soil. They know what to do.

6. Q. When is the compost done?
   A. When earthworms invade the pile and fat robins
   hang around for an easy meal. Some people let their
   compost finish completely, run it through a screen,
   really making it a difficult and tedious job. Composting
   is fun and easy.

Watering

Most people do not need to be told to water their garden and lawns,
but many do not realize the dual importance of adequate moisture. Plants
need water to survive and grow, but so do earthworms. If the ground is
allowed to dry out too extensively, the earthworms will die. Their egg
cases will survive and hatch during the fall rainy season, too late to
benefit the garden for that season. If the ground dries out and the
earthworms die, then relief from drought will have a lesser effect without
the full population of Lumbricids. A sudden shower will not infiltrate as
deeply once tunneling has stopped. The loss of earthworms also means
a reduction in the aerating and fertilizing effects of tunneling and
excretion.

Watering for an hour at a time is minimal both for the garden and the
lawn. To reduce waste, a drip hose can be used to keep more water near
the plants and in the soil.

The Wormhaven Garden.3 will have a barrel to catch rain water from
the church roof.

THREE

Garden Ecology - The Birds and the Bees

Biological Centers of Influence (BCI)

I n the business world, a certified public accounter is a center of influence because of all the businesses and affluent clients he advises. In the garden, a biological center of influence (BCI) is something which changes the habitat of the yard so much that it positively affects many different species at once.

Compost as a BCI

The earthworm-oriented gardener will have already taken the first step in attracting an army of insect eaters in his yard. The compost pit is a breeding ground for centipedes, millipedes, pillbugs, and earthworms. It is a biological center of influence which will affect many kinds of animals by providing food in abundance. Jays and robins will nest near a food source and make the yard their territory. The decision to compost will change the environment of the yard by increasing organic matter rather than disposing of it. The bacteria count in the soil will grow. "One gram of loam from the surface of fertile prairie may contain as many as 2,000,000 protozoans and 58,000,000 bacteria on which some of those protozoans feed." Beneficial molds will flourish. When the microorganism population explodes from building up the humus supply in the yard, then all the animals which depend on the lower creatures will grow in number as well.

God's plan for His Creation is revealed in the way in which the entire population grows in balance, due to the complex relationships between prey and predator, food and eater. The gardener does not need to plan for bluejays. They will arrive. So will cardinals, nuthatches, and chickadees. He may not like sparrows, grackles, and starlings, but they will arrive and work their Master's plan.

Water as a BCI

Every yard has a birdbath, planned or unplanned. A dip in the concrete driveway will hold water for baths and drinks. The lowest place in the yard will form a pond first and hold water during the rainy season. At Wormhaven.3 in New Ulm, the flat roof over the church kitchen holds water in shallow puddles, high above feline predators. When other areas are iced over, these puddles are melted from the sun's energy absorbed by the black asphalt roof. The builders put rails around the edge of the roof, convenient places for birds to land and survey for danger, to rest and preen their miraculous feathers.

Dripping water will attract birds and other wild animals. A large amount of water is especially appealing, since it can support life and store the sun's energy. People who build ponds in their yard will attract wildlife in greater numbers. Simply putting up a birdbath will change the ecology of the yard. Multiple birdbaths will increase the bird population and even attract hawks, who also need to drink and eat. The hawk will pick out the sick birds and make meals out of them, helping the bird population grow stronger.

A birdbath warmer in the winter is a great investment. For about $45 one can obtain a warmer which will keep the water at 40 degrees, enough to stay liquid without using up a lot of energy. The warmer will not shock birds. Animals can obtain the moisture they need from snow, but drinking snow lowers the body temperature. They also need to bathe, so a garbage can lid full of water is inviting both for bathing and drinking. Their feathers repel water, so they can leave the water without freezing solid.

The colder the weather, the more appealing the heated bird spa. I drove up the driveway at Wormhaven.1 in Midland and saw 50 birds lined up to take a bath, in pairs, each pair being pushed out by the pair in line behind them. Many times the birds went through a gallon of water a day on the coldest day. The dirt in the water each time proved that they needed the bath as much as they wanted it.

Squirrels, dogs, and cats will also drop by for a drink of water. One neighborhood cat used to sit next to the birdbath in the summer and pretend to sleep. Not one bird was fooled. Not one bird landed. Some bird lovers hate cats and squirrels, but they are simply following the role assigned by their Creator.

A high pitched dripping noise, to attract birds, can be created by hanging a leaky milk bottle or pail above the birdbath. People also buy fountains and misters which appeal to the birds' hearing and style of bathing. People should not be discouraged from increasing the water supply by the expense. Garbage can lids make fine birdbaths, which can be kept warm with daily doses of hot water. A nail hole in a gallon milk jug will provide just enough dripping to last a day or two.

Water is most important center of influence in the yard, the easiest to create, the cheapest to provide. The animal population in the yard will be in direct proportion to the amount of water provided. Without the proper level of moisture, the compost pile dries out and and dies out, reducing the number of animals supported by the compost. The whole food chain relies on water and will shift to where water is clean, flowing, noisy, and abundant.

Trees as BCI

Trees have many different effects upon the yard. They attract birds by fruiting and by sheltering insects. In the winter their bark harbors insect larvae, providing food for birds, unless an ice storm armor-coats the tree. In the summer the pumping of water from the soil to the leaves creates a miniature air conditioning system around them. Evaporation of gallons of water from the leaves and the shade cast by the tree will influence animal and human life. In addition, each fallen leaf provides food and shade for the soil creatures. Each fallen branch establishes a banquet center for all forms of life, depending on its size.

The Wormhaven gardens never despise the food created by God's nuclear blast furnace, the sun, whether it be weeds, leaves, spoiled fruit, branches, or logs. Most of the food in a plant is from the sun and created by photosynthesis. The soil adds minerals, but the chief energy source is the sun, not the earth. Therefore, every plant is really an addition to the soil when it dies. A weed is a congealed shaft of sunlight, enriched by minerals from the soil. Logs and branches from trees contain even more energy, but it takes longer to get the energy transferred back into the soil.

Any schoolboy knows that a log half-buried in soil will rot fairly soon. How many think about the fungus which attacks and softens the wood, the soil creatures which swarm around and live under the log, the mammals making a home in the log, and the birds seeking food in the concentration of rot? Every log left on the ground is not only a bird feeder, but also a soil fertilizer. Those who want to build up the population of insect eaters in the yard will want to save or bring in logs, to place inconspicuously under the cover of raspberry canes or other tall plants. A brush pile by itself will be a beacon of welcome to mammals, a sanctuary for insects, and a choir loft for birds.

> This is my Father's world;
> The birds their carols raise;
> The morning light, the lily white,
> Declare their Maker's praise.
> (Maltbie Davenport Babcock, 1858-1901)

Bushes and Vines as BCI

When we see a row of tall bushes, especially evergreens, we should see an apartment complex for birds. In God's plan one species will seldom colonize and dominate an area, except for such social birds as purple martins and barn swallows. Instead, a pair of birds stake a claim on a given area and protect that area from their own species by having the male sing loud war-songs which fill the air with the sweetest sound of spring. The robin's song really means, "Get out, all robins. I was here first." If God gave birds the personality and voices of the ugly, brutish Tasmanian devil, we would loathe spring and pray for winter.

Many bushes flower and fruit, offering food to birds, throughout the winter in many cases. Some birds favor a given plant. For instance, holly will attract mockingbirds, who love the berries. At Wormhaven.1 in Midland, hummingbirds darted out of the honeysuckle bushes to dine on scarlet runner bean flowers. Shy cardinals flashed brilliant red as they bathed in the distant birdbath near their nuptial hideaway.

Vines normally fruit, although we seldom value the fruit as much as birds do. The Japanese ivy which festoons Yale's pseudo-gothic buildings in New Haven and my neo-Minnesota garage in New Ulm is a type of grape. A riot of vines between my neighbor's garage and mine has created a year-around habitat for birds. The sparrows often launch their attack

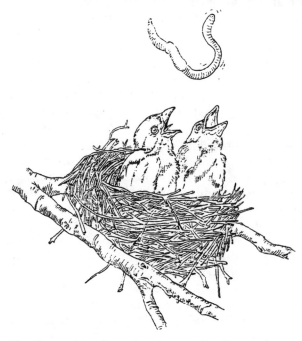

on the bird feeding station from the vines, going first to the mock orange bush, then to the branches I placed on the flat kitchen roof, finally to the seed on the roof itself.

Trees and bushes are used to support flowering vines, which will add color to the base plant and food for wildlife. A trumpet vine with orange flowers will draw hummingbirds with its nectar. Roses will climb into a prosaic maple and bloom. Every gardener can have his own Laocoon by letting a vine snake through a bush or tree.

Birds in the Garden

Once a gardener learns to appreciate earthworms, attention will then turn to other easy and inexpensive methods of improving garden ecology, to provide a haven where God's servants work according to His plan. Insects have a knack for finding their food in the garden, but most insects are not harmful. A few thousand species give the rest a bad reputation. In the same way, the rapacity and cleverness of the corvids (bluejays and crows) have led to some unfair remarks about their extended family.

Grackles, starlings, sparrows, and wrens get very little acclaim. Like weeds, the birds which flourish get no credit for doing their job well. All garden birds, including crows and jays, consume vast amounts of insects, weed seeds, or both. A chickadee will make thousands of trips in one day to feed insects and grubs to her young. A bluejay can spot a beetle yards away and pounce on him. Starlings and mourning doves work the lawn and garden over with a thoroughness that inspires awe. I have seen a grackle poke his strong beak into the watered lawn 15 times looking for grubs (and aerating the grass). Imagine what a flock of grackles can do!

Grackles tend to associate with starlings. Both kinds are extremely wary ground feeders, comical, and smart. Once I was sitting in the back yard at twilight when a grackle landed near me and started to forage in the lawn. He moved steadily toward me, intent on the potential for food in the ground. Up in the tree, his spouse Martha noticed his increasing danger. She called, "Ralph." He fluffed his feathers in irritation and responded, "Coming!" Instead, he moved closer to me. The call got more insistent, "Ralph!" Taking more time, he puffed up, stuck out his head, replied, "Coming!" and went on searching for a last tidbit. He was within six feet of me when a virtual shriek came, "RALPH!" Looking up, he finally noticed me, but did not want to appear absentminded. He quietly foraged back to a safe spot and took off to receive a thorough dressing down for his careless behavior.

The gardener who understands biological centers of influence will provide water and shelter before he worries about buying food for birds. God has cared for His creatures since the beginning, and they will live without our help.

> Behold the fowls of the air: for they sow not, neither do they reap, nor gather into barns; yet your heavenly Father feedeth them. Are ye not much better than they? (Matthew 6:26)

Jesus not only taught us that God provides for His creatures, but also that we are far more precious in His sight. (Matthew 10:29)

We began feeding birds simply by saving scraps from the dinner table. Pizza crusts, soggy grapes, bread crumbs, peanuts, and sources of fat were left on a silverware tray which we nailed to a post near the kitchen window. Morning meant two things. The crows which fed on the ground flew up into the trees as soon as they heard a sound in the kitchen. Then the bluejay appeared on the silverware tray, soaking wet from his morning bath, and screamed, "Jay! Jay!" at me. He wanted me to put peanuts on the tray for him and seemed very angry when I failed to comply with his demands.

People insist that we must continue feeding birds once we start, or they will starve to death after being spoiled. Birds simply move on to another food source, and they definitely prefer God's menu to anything we can provide. Activity at the bird feeder always drops off when the spring bugs arrive. Food will attract more birds and a greater variety to the yard. In the winter, food will mean that more birds will survive extreme cold and ice storms. Water and shelter will still be more significant throughout the year than food.

Attracting a few more birds to the yard is not only entertaining but useful as well. Most birds eat some insects and concentrate on them during spring, when God planned for the demands of baby birds to reduce the population of pests. Then the harried parents spend all their time seeking enough food for their famished broods. If the birds nest in the yard, they will look for insects in the garden, in trees and bushes, under every leaf and gob of mulch.

Hanging suet (kidney fat from cows) on trees and bushes in produce bags will attract the birds which especially like insects: chickadees, woodpeckers, nuthatches, starlings, and grackles. A bag of suet costs a little over a dollar and lasts all winter. Our front yard nuthatches (called upside-down birds, for their habit of seeking insects in bark by moving upside down) at Wormhaven.3 squeak in pleasure when they land on the suet and peck at it. If they depended on human food alone, they would never leave the suet. Instead, they visit it several times a day in the winter.

To illustrate how little God's creatures value our judgment, let me offer one example. I bought a special nut-enhanced suet from a supply company for 250% the cost of plain suet. The recipe sounded delicious to me, and it smelled wonderful when I unwrapped it. I pictured flocks of birds waiting in line for their gourmet suet. However, no bird was ever seen on it, since they preferred the plain suet a few feet away. Our front yard squirrel visited the nutty suet and devoured it in several sittings, chewing open the bag and enjoying all the peanuts and fat inside. Each of his meals cost me about 50 cents. Outsmarted, I bought him a cheaper feeding station, a little chair near a spike which holds an ear of field corn. He sits politely on his chair, outside my office window, and enjoys corn twice a day, his paws folded in pious devotion to His Creator.

Suet is the least expensive food for a variety of birds, but sunflower seeds will attract the most species. Because they are high in nutrition and calories, sunflower seeds will be appreciated by: cardinals, grosbeaks, chickadees, nuthatches, bluejays, finches, sparrows and starlings. Squirrels love sunflower seeds as well, but do not like safflower seeds or thistle seeds. Many towns now have stores which specialize in wild birds, so it is possible to get one kind of seed at a time rather than grocery store mixes. When in doubt, hang several bags of suet and buy black oil sunflower seeds. Sunflower seeds are eaten by 42 species of American birds.

Once we attended a gymnastics show where the sponsors overestimated their need for popcorn. We dragged home two man-sized bags of popcorn at the fire sale price of $4, just in time for a March 31st snowstorm. Each day we scattered popcorn in the snow and put some in a wire bunbasket in the maple tree. Each day, crows, starlings, and grackles flocked in to feast. The starlings were so delighted with the arrangement that they stayed in the Christmas trees we had gathered and propped up as bird shelter. Each time I came out in the yard, the starlings gave an avian cheer, "There he is! The popcorn man!" It was so much fun feeding them that I wondered whether I was giving or receiving Pavlovian conditioning. They stayed around in the spring and did a fine job of scouting the garden for insects. Theater popcorn was always saved for the garden, to entice the birds.

Birds will call attention to themselves when they see the person who feeds them. Many stories are told of birds being tuned to the sound of a particular car engine coming home from work. Squirrels are no less habitual and habit forming. I was raking the leaves in the front yard when I had the prickly feeling of being watched. When I turned around, I saw the squirrel which I had been feeding for weeks from a bag of English walnuts, a gift from another gardener. He sat up, looking hungry. I said, "Wait there and I will get you something." I went inside the house and grabbed an apple. He waited for me to return, so I rolled the apple up to him. He looked at it with disgust and refused to eat. I said, "I'm sorry. I'll get you a walnut." I went in a second time and got a walnut. He waited again. When he got his treat, he spun it in his paws, checking for flaws, and scampered off to bury it.

When a squirrel was struck on the street in front of our house, my wife claimed it was one of my overfed pets who could not run fast enough or else suffered a heart attack from a rich diet of cookies and walnuts. However, she also fed cookies to our backyard squirrel when I pointed out that the animal begging on the bird feeder was obviously a nursing mother. I asked in the tone of a prosecutor, "Would you deny cookies to a mommy squirrel?"

Some gardeners think of birds as their enemies, since birds will eat cherries, strawberries, and raspberries. They are forgetting the old rhyme:

One for the blackbird,
One for the mouse,
One for the squirrel,
One for the house.

If someone moves out to the woods, clears some land, and plants four strawberries plants, three raspberry canes, and one cherry tree, he should not be surprised that all of God's creation will land on those beautiful red fruits the moment they are ripe. How many times did I go to check on our luscious blackberries, only to find a chipmunk running back to his hole with the latest one? How can I forget my very first home grown raspberry, which ripened three seconds before the bluejay ate it? If we plant in abundance, God's creatures will eat with some discretion and leave plenty for us. St. Paul said it well:

> But this I say, He which soweth sparingly shall reap also sparingly; and he which soweth bountifully shall reap also bountifully. (2 Corinthians 9:6)

Gardeners will enjoy their work if they plant enough to take care of their helpers and themselves, but not so much that the work becomes a burden.

The Wormhaven gardener will want to feed as many birds as possible,

through plantings and rotten logs, since they love God's food and eat for free, more or less. Raspberries are a great crop for birds and humans, easy to raise, delightful for both species. Sunflowers are easy to grow and packed with food for birds and squirrels alike. We saw one swaying wildly as a squirrel clung to it upside down, eating away at the giant seed head. A variety of fruiting plants and trees will make birds happy.

Mulch

I first mulched with grass clippings to conserve water for raspberries, later to feed the earthworms as well. Still later, I learned that mulch helped the birds find food. The ground is always soft and moist under mulch, teeming with life. Soil creatures love moist rot and hate sun, so they are just below any thick layer of mulch. Many different insects work on mulch, and earthworms pull it down for food. Birds simply poke their beaks into the mulch and pull out their dinner. I have seen mourning doves, who enjoy weed seeds, slowly pacing through the mulched rows of the garden. Bluejays and robins will perch on the fence, waiting for telltale movement of lower life forms. Sparrows and starlings will join the hunt, especially when they are used to finding bread products and popcorn in the garden. Starlings stalk along with a comical gait and flip mulch away with their beaks. They can then grab an insect before it buries itself in the soil.

Slugs may inhabit a mulched garden, since they too love moisture, shade, and rot. Unfortunately, most birds do not consider them good eating. Slug predators are the garter snake and toads. We built Toad Hall, an upside down flower pot, for our first toad, Freckles. Toads love shade and plenty of water. A pond in the yard is a good habitat for toads, as long as they have shade as well. Garter snakes should always be welcome in the garden and imported, if possible.

Slugs can be trapped under shingles during the day and destroyed. Like their human counterparts, they will drown themselves in beer. Gardeners should not become overly concerned with slugs. A soggy season will boost the slug population; a drought will decimate them... and the garden.

Beneficial Insects and Related Helpers

The best way to deal with harmful insects in the garden is to ignore them and let God's assault force take over. Birds, spiders, and other

insects will reduce insect pests to a tolerable level. If a large number of pests appear, it is a feast for the predator who specializes in that insect. For instance, when the cottony maple scale appeared on our maple tree, so did thousands of lady bugs and extra birds. The maple tree survived. Later I learned that malathion spraying against mosquitos boosted the maple scale population by killing the beneficial insects, such as lady bugs, along with butterflies and moths. Man cannot kill insects with discrimination, while God can reduce pests while increasing the attractive, beneficial creatures.

I did not use pesticides from the beginning, because of my desire to see the balance of forces at work in God's creation. Insect damage was never serious, except on a stand of asparagus, one of our favorite foods. When I saw that the asparagus beetle had stripped my planting, I went

73

looking for a can of anything toxic to use on them. But, when I came out of the house, our son Martin, age 10, had stained his fingers bright green with insect gore. "They are all dead, Dad. I squished them."

Another stand of asparagus had some damage, which stopped at the point where a praying mantis stood on guard, arms folded as if asking God for another beetle. The mantis was the offspring of eggs cases bought from Henry Field, for $1 each. The mantis has weaknesses, such as leaving the egg case and devouring his siblings as they emerge. A praying mantis will stay in the yard where he hatches, if he escapes the jaws of his relatives.

Henry Field also offers lace wings and other predators known as beneficial parasites. They are fun to buy and try out, especially if children are around as an excuse for spending the money. "It's educational!" will work on reluctant spouses who wonder why it is necessary to buy insect predators. Our praying mantis went to school in a glass jar and spooked all the children. They were hypnotized by the sinister turn of his alien head as he tried to stare down the children, as if they were food.

One reason to avoid insecticides in the garden, besides killing off the beneficial insects, is the prospect of eating the same toxins which made the pests fall over dead. The cost is high and never stops, since new pests will step in over the bodies of their relatives, without insect predators to stop them. The result of letting God's assault forces do my work for free has been minimal insect damage. Hungry boys will do more to a garden in 10 minutes than insects can do in a century. It is fun to watch them enjoy fresh produce from the garden, knowing it is packed with vitamins, minerals, but safe to eat. A tomato warm from the sun, a tender young carrot, a crunchy spinach leaf, a sugary pea pod: no child should grow up without such delights.

Our squirrel also enjoys a little gardening. I found him running his rodentine paws along the Lincoln pea vines, harvesting the peas for himself.

The Bees and Their Ornery Relatives

Corn pollinates with the wind, but most plants need help from the bees. These highly organized creatures are absolutely necessary for most garden plants and fruits. They are harmless to normal people and only sting those who flail at them and shout. When a bee of any type is in my way in the garden, I brush him aside with my bare hands. They never sting.

Watching bees can be very relaxing. They love to hover around clover and hollyhocks, two plants which are always in bloom. Their arrival on raspberry and blackberry flowers is a sign that fruit is not far away.

Yellow jackets like to dig a hole in the lawn and attack the person who dares to mow over their home. Boiling water in their nest will discourage them. One person put molasses in their hole, knowing a skunk would come by and have sweetened yellow jackets for supper.

Wasps and hornets prey upon pests, so they are good, even if a little short tempered.

Companion Planting

Some knowledge of companion planting will help in avoiding some common mistakes. Opposites help one another in the garden, just as they do in marriage. Plants of the same family should not be placed together, because they will thwart each other. The best books on this subject are Louise Riotte's *Roses Love Garlic* and her companion volume *Carrots Love Tomatoes*.

I have asked married couples about how they squeeze toothpaste from a tube, how neat they are, and how they arrive at airports. The grim facts are: bottom squeezers of tubes marry top squeezers, neatniks marry slobs, and someone who wants to be two hours early always pairs up with someone who runs down the airport corridor 10 minutes late. Nevertheless, these opposing characteristics—while causing spouses to shout, "You drive me nuts!"—will also make them very successful if they are faithful to the Word and to each other.

Nightshades do not get along. They are: potatoes, green peppers, tomatoes, egg plant, tobacco, deadly nightshade, and woody nightshade.

Umbrella seed heads (umbellifers) thwart one another. They are: carrot, dill, queen-ann's-lace (or wild carrot), parsley, and fennel.

Cucurbits do not like to grow together. They are: cucumbers, gourds, pumpkins, and squash.

The garlic family (allium) includes garlic, onions, and chives.

Brassicas are cabbage, broccoli, brussels sprouts, and mustard greens.

Plant families are easy to identify from the similarity of their flowers and fruit. The nightshades are all related to deadly nightshade, the source of belladonna, still used in medicine. The bright red berry of the woody nightshade is a smaller version of the tomato, but as poisonous as the black berry of the deadly nightshade. It is not surprising that the tomato was grown as an ornamental long before it was eaten, given the reputation of its deadly nightshade cousin.

Plant families have similar pests and diseases. Our Uncle Henry Stickl asked why his tomatoes looked so bad after using his tobacco plants as mulch on them. His tomatoes were wilted and sick looking. I pointed out that tobacco carries the same wilt disease which affects tomatoes. It is fine to mulch with the **same** plant but not with a similar plant. Uncle Henry was impressed that a city boy understood gardening.

Companion planting means putting plants together which tend to ward off pests and diseases from each other. Garlic is good with almost everything except cousins chive and onion. I would never plant roses without garlic growing nearby, and I never hesitate to plant garlic as many places as possible. Garlic can be planted in the fall or spring. Each clove will turn into a bulb and then will create a fairy ring of garlic if not dug up in time. The value of garlic comes from the strong chemicals given off by the plant, which repel insects and seem to strengthen other plants.

Tomatoes are good with asparagus and with basil. If someone plants one huge area of tomatoes, they will serve as a landing beacon for every pest which preys upon them, drawn by the sight and smell of them. Breaking up the mass with other plants will dilute the "Come and Get It!" signal to pests and help the opposites strengthen each other. (See the recipe for basil, asparagus, and tomato at the end of the book.)

Rabbits and Earthworms

Those who want to raise the ideal Wormhaven pet will find it surprisingly simple. Rabbit owners and former rabbit breeders are everywhere. Advice and books are easy to obtain. Proper equipment includes an all-wire cage, a feeding dish which cannot be tipped, and a watering bottle. Feed can be purchased at a hardware store, pet store, or grain elevator. The equipment is often available second-hand.

Rabbits do not bay at the moon; they do not swing from the new curtains or fish for food in the aquarium. Rabbits are cleaner than cats, gentle and loving, but do not demand attention. Our Siamese cats used to wake us up in the morning with their hellish yowling, first bawling in our ears, then in our faces, so we could smell their fish breath. Rabbits do not need obedience school, a license, or shots. They do not carry any diseases while alive. (Dead rabbits can harbor tularemia, but one can hardly blame a corpse for that!) Rabbit sitters are easier to hire than dog or cat sitters.

Rabbits can be kept outdoors, in a garage, or even in the house. Our rabbits lived in the garage because it kept the yard neater. Rabbits do have a few preferences. They like some privacy, so we kept a blanket or hideaway in each cage. Our buck, Popcorn, often ate his meal with the blanket covering most of his body. But rabbits also like a good view, so a wire cage allows them to look around. Rabbits are very clean and prefer one end of the cage for elimination. A wire cage allows their urine and droppings to go into a container. A board in the cage gives them something more comfortable to sit on. They lick themselves almost constantly and help groom one another.

A female rabbit will use her strong head to sweep the other does away from the food. I saw a mother brush her daughter to one side, only to see me watching. She immediately began grooming her daughter. It was difficult to tell whether she was trying to play innocent or just following the instinct to feed, and then to clean. When two rabbits shared a long dandelion flower, chewing toward the middle, one ended the race with a quick turn of her head, pulling the stem from her sister's mouth.

Rabbits need a lot of clean water, especially in the summer. They have no trouble staying warm, but they can die of heat in the summer. Pastor Vance Fossum is famous for leaving a conference phone call, yelling, "The parsonage is on fire!" A child tried to keep the bunnies warm in the winter with a space heater and ignited the wood siding of the home. The fire was quickly extinguished, but the story will never be forgotten in the Church of the Lutheran Confession. We visited the historic site in St. Louis, at Faith Lutheran Church on Big Bend Road. Pastor Mark Gullerud pointed to the place where the fire started.

Rabbits love snacks from the garden. Ours enjoyed strawberry, rose, raspberry, dandelion, plantain, and comfrey leaves. Some plants are considered medicinal for rabbits, but it is difficult to tell which ones work at a given time. Rabbits do not respond to the same treatment the same way. Our rabbits liked to eat carrot tops, but not carrots, in spite of the Bugs Bunny legend.

Our rabbit population zoomed soon after we added our buck, Popcorn. First we bought Joy from a student at school. Then a church member found Pride cornered by her dogs. Pride was obviously a pet, since she cuddled so well. We bought our doe Galadriel at a show and then received Popcorn as a gift. Four rabbits added up to 10 in a short time.

Rabbit manure became a problem very quickly with 10 animals in 3 cages. My wife thought of buying children's swimming pools to catch the waste. I decided to add red wiggler earthworms and soil to the pools, to complete the nitrogen cycle. Rabbits have a very high nitrogen content in their droppings and urine. That is good for the green growth of plants, but bad for the ammonia which is quickly generated. We learned that hoeing the droppings under the soil and adding some soil was enough to keep odor down and reduce the flies. Spiders set up shop in the garage, and their webs became coated with ambient rabbit hair, giving the webs a haunted house look.

When I dug soil out of the swimming pools for the garden, I had shovels of earthworms, thousands of them, coiled together and ready to work. Plenty of egg cases came out with each pile of soil. Normally, I cleaned out half of each pool and filled it with fresh soil. That gave the earthworms in the other half a chance to multiply in fresh soil. One way we used the earthworm/manure combination was to dig trenches in garden areas and fill them. The soil was quickly blended by the earthworms.

Hot manure (high in nitrogen) is good for getting compost going, so some manure went into the compost pile. The dry droppings were easy to scatter in the garden and the lawn. I knew earthworms would transform the droppings into castings and multiply. Meanwhile, we reduced our purchase of rabbit food by giving the rabbits meals from garden leftovers. They fed the earthworms which fed the plants which fed them. We also think that wild rabbits left our yard alone because of the aroma of so much competition. Rabbits are territorial and mark their

1995

turf with urine and chin glands.

For those who want baby bunnies (properly called kittens), a nest box is needed, plus a buck and doe. Readers should obtain some rabbit books before breeding. The newborns are quite vulnerable, so it is easy to lose a few litters at first. We lost two litters, then had Elrond, Frodo, Arwin, and Aragorn. It was a special treat for us and our neighbors to see the soft white hair pulled from Galadriel's dewlap (a double chin on females) blanketing the kittens on cold mornings and opening up as the day warmed up. The bunnies, born naked, soon furred out and relied less and less on their mother's fur comforter to keep them warm.

Children love rabbits and learn a lot about their Creator from them. They see the love of the mother for her kittens, the rapid growth of the bunnies, the instinctive behavior which protects them, the amazing radar-antennae ears, and their need for shelter, food, and water. Lovable rabbits give parents many opportunities to teach their children about God's Creation.

We had our rabbit named Joy pay a visit to our daughter Erin Joy, who was helpless from a neurological degenerative disorder. Erin was weak and could not speak or even roll over on her own, but she loved feeling the soft fur of Joy against her hands and feet. Erin enjoyed hearing about her visit with Martin's pet, because everything her brother did was perfect in her eyes. Erin, like her sister Bethany, died very young, filled with the grace of God.[23]

The more we garden, the more we see how all of the created plants and animals work together in one grand Hallelujah Chorus in the garden.

> For by him were all things created, that are in heaven, and that are in earth, visible and invisible, whether they be thrones, or dominions, or principalities, or powers: all things were created by him, and for him: and he is before all things, and by him all things consist. And he is the head of the body, the church: who is the beginning, the firstborn from the dead; that in all things he might have the preeminence. (Colossians 1:16-18)

God creates order rather than disorder. When tragic events are difficult to understand, the garden reminds us of what the Holy Spirit teaches us in the Word of God. Everything has a purpose, and we are never forgotten by our heavenly Father. "Are not two sparrows sold for a farthing? and one of them shall not fall on the ground without your Father." (Matthew 10:29)

FOUR

Beautiful Flowers, Easy to Grow

ardening is more enjoyable when it is easy and productive, but no one minds a little work when the neighbors are overwhelmed by the beauty of the flowers. When the basic principles of Creation are understood, the gardener is overwhelmed with the knowledge that he does perhaps 1 percent of the work while God does the rest. Indeed, most of the work is accomplished while the gardener is asleep, as the parable, unique to Mark, teaches:

> And he said, So is the kingdom of God, as if a man should cast seed into the ground; {27} And should sleep, and rise night and day, and the seed should spring and grow up, he knoweth not how. {28} For the earth bringeth forth fruit of herself; first the blade, then the ear, after that the full corn in the ear. {29} But when the fruit is brought forth, immediately he putteth in the sickle, because the harvest is come. (Mark 4:26-29)

Parallels between the growth of Christianity and growth in God's Creation are common in the New Testament.

The forces of Creation remain a mystery to us, no matter how much we study them. Paul's statement about this is a hymn of praise:

> O the depth of the riches both of the wisdom and knowledge of God! how unsearchable are his judgments, and his ways past

finding out! {34} For who hath known the mind of the Lord? or who hath been his counsellor? {35} Or who hath first given to him, and it shall be recompensed unto him again? {36} For of him, and through him, and to him, are all things: to whom be glory for ever. Amen. (Romans 11:33-36)

The first thing we can do to grow beautiful flowers is to begin with the best seed, stock, or bulbs. This is where so many gardeners fail.

Notice the parallel. All the blessings of the Christian faith come from God acting through His Word. The Holy Spirit makes people sorrow for their sins through the power of the Word. The Holy Spirit gives them faith through the Word to receive the Good News that Christ has died for their sins and risen from the dead. The Holy Spirit preserves their faith through the Word so that they will join the saints in heaven when they die. Therefore, every single blessing in the life of a Christian begins with God in His energetic and effective Word. When believers blossom and flourish, they do so because of the Word, the source of the fruits of faith.

To grow beautiful flowers, we do not look for the end product, the blooms, but for the source, the best seed, stock, and bulbs. C. F. W. Walther wrote:

Pay more attention to pure life, and you will raise a growth of genuine Christianity." That is exactly like saying to a farmer: "Do not worry forever about good seed; worry about good fruits." Is not a farmer properly concerned about good fruit when he is solicitous about getting good seed? Just so a concern about pure doctrine is the proper concern about genuine Christianity and a sincere Christian life. False doctrine is noxious seed, sown by the enemy to produce a progeny of wickedness. The pure doctrine is wheat-seed; from it spring the children of the Kingdom, who even in the present life belong in the kingdom of Jesus Christ and in the life to come will be received into the Kingdom of Glory. 1

Unfortunately, this is where most gardeners self-destruct. They look at the hobby as their work rather than God's, so they overlook the principles of Creation.

Hardy Bulbs: Tulips, Daffodils, Allium, Hyacinth, and Crocus

If I could promise you a flower every time you planted, would you take the time to plant a few bulbs? A true bulb actually is a flower already, wrapped in its organic cocoon, alive and full of power. The only requirement of a bulb to bloom is being planted right-side-up. Hardy bulbs, planted in the fall, take root and grow toward the surface, then stop, waiting for spring. They prove that winter is not a time of death but dormancy, sleeping beneath a blanket of snow. Bulbs burst into bloom when spirits are sagging from too long a winter. They give the gardener a running start on the season by bringing neighbors to his yard to admire the beauty and repent for their lack of diligence the previous fall. Fall bulbs offer so much enjoyment for so little work.

The gardener who respects Creation and worships the Creator will naturally be at work in the fall. All the organic material is stored in the compost pile, to let God's creatures work during the winter. The weather is perfect for gardening in the fall, and dreamers can imagine what next year's bounty will be like, without suffering from too much reality breaking in. He can plant bulbs with perfect confidence in the results he will get, not from his minimal work but from God's design and purpose.

The first step is to order a catalog from the best supplier:

Dutch Gardens
P. O. Box 200
Adelphia, NJ 07710
Phone: 908-780-2713
Fax: 908-780-7720.

The congregations I serve always have a group order, which gives the church a bonus of free bulbs for around the church lot. After ordering bulbs from many suppliers, I found that Dutch Gardens offers much larger bulbs at much better prices. A larger bulb has more food supply and will produce better flowers.

Hardy (or fall) bulbs are those which need to be chilled in the ground in order to bloom in the spring. They can be left in the ground. Some popular hardy bulbs are: tulips, daffodils, hyacinth, iris, allium, crocus, snow glories, snow drops, and grape hyacinths.

Tender (or spring) bulbs will not tolerate a severe chill and need to be dug up each year and stored for the winter. Some tender bulbs are: dahlia, gladiolus, begonia, and canna. Lilies, daylilies, and oriental lilies are hardy, but they are often sold with the spring bulbs. Many of the plants listed above are not true bulbs, but the term is loosely applied to anything which is not a seed or a seedling. If someone calls a gladiolus corm a bulb, it is not considered polite to correct him at a meeting of the garden club, or even in the privacy of his back yard.

Fall Bulbs

It is better to begin with a few drifts of bulbs and see how they work out, before ordering enough for an estate. The idea is not to plant a rainbow mixture of bulbs but to get a mass of color or a contrast between two colors.

Tulips

Tulips have been developed for so long that one can buy almost any color and size and vary the blooming time. They are loved for their beauty and variety but have two flaws. One is that they do not multiply in the soil but fade away unless dug up and babied. The other flaw is their attractiveness as food. They can be boiled and eaten like onions, something the Dutch were forced to do in World Ware II, but they are usually eaten raw by deer and other animals. Nevertheless, tulips at their best are tall, royal, egg-shaped flowers of exquisite beauty.

I plant Darwin tulips because they are very tall, up to 30 inches, and will last longer in the soil. I do not like to dig them up, because I plant small bulbs on the layer above them, to double the flower power in each hole. When hardy bulbs are finally dug up, the small bulbs can be divided and replanted. People often start with new tulip bulbs every few years, but the small bulbs keep growing and multiplying.

Some tulip types are: triumph (16-18 inches tall; mid-spring flowering); greigii (8 inches tall, early spring flowering), fosteriana (12-14 inches tall, early spring flowering); botanicals (wild tulips cultivated for their unusual flowers); parrot (ruffled petals, late spring flowering, 18-20 inches tall); lily flowered (22-24 inches tall, late spring flowering); and peony tulips (18-20 inches tall, late spring flowering). One could easily fill the yard with a wide selection of tulip types.

This is how to leave an impression with tulips. Plan an area to hold 25-50 bulbs, all of the same variety and color. Dig it out down to 7 inches deep early in the fall. If the soil is sandy, mix it with compost and old manure. Fresh manure would not be good because it would damage to the bulbs. Add fireplace ashes or bulb booster to the bottom of the hole and mix it around. The bulbs are going to be sitting down there for a few years, and they need plenty of food. Next place the bulbs in the hole a few inches apart. Shovel soil onto them and pack it around the bulbs. Once they are completely covered, add a layer of crocus, all the same variety and color.

Some bulb booster may be added when the crocus are covered up. Water should be added to remove air pockets in the soil and to give the roots a good start.

In the spring, the crocus will first send up their tiny striped leaves. They will bloom first and fade away. Then the tulips will send their leaves up through the soil, soon after the gardener thinks they all died in the winter. The pointed tips appear first and give the impression of Venus rising from the sea as they reach up. When the tulips are in full bloom, a few may be cut and brought inside. But tulips are best as outdoor flowers, cheering the neighborhood with their stately elegance. The best bulbs have been cultivated in Holland, not Michigan, and show their good breeding.

The gardener who bought bulbs the previous fall from a rose company, hardware or discount store will dig the same hole and even use various soil amendments (compost, manure, bulb booster). But he will be stuck with the blooms of feeble, diseased, starved bulbs of uncertain origin. Something colorful will emerge from that hole, to mock his poor judgment and remind him that his neighbor did not worry about the flower but the bulb. But the bloom of his bargain bulb will be small, droopy, and lack the purity of the perfect bulbs planted down the street. Once a bargain bulb buyer knows the difference, he will never want anything but the best bulbs in his yard, and he will not mix low quality bulbs with top quality bulbs. He will be adamant, knowing that it is not the gardener but the bulb.

How then, we ask, can Christians be so deceived that they seek a tall steeple, plush carpets, and parking lots larger than the Great Plains, all from a word of uncertain origin, not the pure Word of God, but the ever-changing and corrupt word of man? How can they patiently listen to an ordained minister who teaches evolution, and then pray to the Creator for His blessing? How can they tolerate the witch grass of "problems with Genesis" without seeing it creep into the New Testament, the Virgin Birth of Christ, His atonement, and His bodily resurrection?

Daffodils

We cannot divorce the beauty of the garden from the Beautifier, Whose intricate designs are woven into the genetic code of every living thing. The daffodil bulb is uncommonly ugly. If animated, it would serve well in a series of horror movies. But the daffodil is toxic to furry animals, multiplies in the soil, and blooms in various shades of yellow, pink, white, and orange. It is not quite as developed commercially as the tulip, but a wide variety of cheerful blooms can be grown.

One never knows what flowers will do to people. I took flowers to work for my wife, Chris, when I dropped her off at DNV Technica in Columbus, Ohio. Daffodils were blooming all over the yard, so I cut a few and left them with my wife. Unknown to us, the daffodil is the flower of Wales, and the founder of the company was Welsh. He was deliriously happy and insisted on having the sunny flowers on his desk that day. "It reminds me of my childhood in Wales," he said.

I order daffodils from Dutch Gardens, and they are usually double or triple bulbs. That means that one or two smaller bulbs have grown from the main bulb and need to be separated before planting. Therefore, buying 10 bulbs means planting at least 20. I plant tulips in drifts near the house and daffodils in front of the trees. I dig a hole for 5-10 daffodil bulbs, dig in compost and bulb booster, plant a layer of crocus above them, and cover them with the sod removed from the hole. I water them, to give them a good start before the freeze.

After buying some of the exotic colors of daffodils, I have decided that plain yellow is good enough in most cases. The center may be orange, or white, or fringed, but these variations are more impressive in huge blow-ups in the catalog. Most people do not look at them from 3 inches away, which is the perspective of the photos in the catalogs. If one wants to grow an unusual variety, such as the pink daffodil called Salome, it is better to have a large planting which will bring out the unusual color.

Daffodils are easy to naturalize, that is, to grow and spread through the lawn. An ambitious person might want to plant and divide daffodils until a large area of the lawn blooms with them each spring. In a small lawn, one could naturalize an exotic and more costly variety, such as a multi-flowered daffodil, or a double variety with twice the petals.

Most people do not take the trouble to plant bulbs in the lawn, so the effect is impressive for being unusual. Garden and hardware stores sell a hand-held device which will cut out a hole in the lawn for the bulb. The bulb is placed at the bottom of the hole with some bulb booster and the plug of turf is dropped on top of it.

Daffodils and tulips should not be allowed to go to seed, since seed formation draws strength from the bulb. The flower should be cut off when it begins to fade. The foliage must remain to feed the bulb for the next year.

Hyacinths

Hyacinths are known for their bottle brush appearance, solid colors, and heavy perfume. They are double the cost of good tulips and daffodils because of the need to build up the bulb for the total bloom of flowerlets the first year. The second year they will not be as filled out, so they need to be ignored or replaced. They may be a better choice for indoor forcing, since their perfume and color make them a novelty. Compared to purchased flowers which fade quickly, forced hyacinths are a bargain.

Crocus and Grape Hyacinth

Crocus and grape hyacinths are small bulbs with small prices. Crocus come in many colors and are also multi-colored. The bulbs are edible but seem to survive the predation of small, cute animals. Crocus have blooms which show up better in the grass and under bushes, but grape hyacinths reproduce at the rate of 25 percent or more per year. If one continues to divide them and shepherd grape hyacinths, a gardener can have a massive planting of hundreds or even thousands, as one friend did over a period of 20 years. The aroma from hundreds of grape hyacinths is so sweet, and the sight is impressive.

Grape hyacinths are not genuine hyacinths, but they look a little like the real thing. Grape hyacinths are ideal for spreading under bushes, near rocks, and under trees. Crocus are my choice for the second story above the big bulbs: tulips, daffodils, and hyacinths. Gardeners do forget where they planted bulbs, and the striped leaves of the crocus are a good reminder of where the large bulbs will come from. Some people will let crocus multiply until the year when leaves come up but no blooms. That means they need to be dug up and divided, because they are too crowded.

Each Wormhaven front lawn has been planted with crocus. It requires discipline to sit in the grass and dig holes in the lawn, drop in some bulb booster, drop in one tiny bulb, water it, and close the hole. Neighbors walk by and make a point of not asking about the project, for fear of hearing about men from Pluto, gamma rays, and the dangers of fluoridation. One hundred crocus bulbs do not fill up a large bag, but 100 holes in the lawn seem like 1,000 near the end! It is difficult not to think of a passage in Hebrews:

Now no chastening for the present seemeth to be joyous, but grievous: nevertheless afterward it yieldeth the peaceable fruit of righteousness unto them which are exercised thereby. {12} Wherefore lift up the hands which hang down, and the feeble knees... (Hebrews 12:11-12)

In the spring, before the grass is mowed, crocus flowers bloom across the lawn and sober the neighbors' thoughts. "So that's what you were doing in the fall. I was afraid to ask."

Faith Lutheran Church in New Ulm has a small front lawn, so I planted brightly colored crocus near the front entrance and fat, purple crocus near the sign. Drifts of crocus will also bloom in the parsonage lawn. I planted 350 bulbs altogether, so spring will be colorful. The members and the neighbors will enjoy their display for weeks before others flowers bloom.

Exotic Bulbs for the Inner Child

We all like to enjoy something different, and bulbs can be a genuine thrill for everyone. What would a child say if he saw a flower stalk 4 feet tall with a globular purple flower on top? Would he walk up to it, test the stalk, look into the complex flower, ask where it came from? The flower is a giant allium, a garlic. The clove from which it comes is almost as big as a man's fist. Garlic will produce the same flower, only much smaller. So will chives. Common allium may also be planted, for a small version of the giant allium. Three giant allium stalks will stop traffic. I will count how many people ask me, "What are those huge purple flowers?"

The similarity of the allium (garlic family) blooms is a good lesson for children, who enjoy learning that God can design a purple flower to be as big as basketball or as small as a marble. Many versions of the same flower argue for a common design from an uncommon Designer.

Another wild-looking flower is the crown imperial, which almost defies description. It is two feet tall, with orange or yellow flowers which hang down from a leafy top. Each flower is bell-shaped and seems to weep, so they are called "crying lilies." They also have a mild skunk-like odor which will penetrate the bulb package. When the group bulb order came to the church and sat in the still air of the hallway, someone asked, "What happened?" The aroma is not foul but distinctive, reputed to drive away rodents and moles. I plant three at a time, either all yellow or all orange. Children enjoy the "crying" and the odd aroma. Adults like the bizarre appearance.

Roses

Roses are the best possible flowers: relatively easy to grow, fairly inexpensive per bloom, and extremely popular as gifts. I have grown them in Michigan, Ohio, and Missouri. In Ohio, we were blessed with constant rain one summer, which prompted so much blooming from the roses that I had to prune them every day. We kept taking roses to Chris' workplace. The men and women loved having roses at their desks. One day a secretary got a dozen roses from her husband. She said to my wife, "Look at what your roses did!" She was so pleased with the regular delivery of roses at work that her husband took notice. He wanted to please her, so he paid as much for one bouquet as five bushes cost me. Roses led to more roses, lifted people's spirits, put a reconstituted sunbeam on each desk, and prompted, on more than one occasion, a lesson from John 15:1-8.

Our next flower order, as I write, is for bare root roses. The two best sources are:

> Fred Edmunds
> 6235 SW Kahle Road
> Wilsonville OR 97070
> Phone: 503-682-1476
> Fax: 503-682-1275

> Jackson and Perkins
> P. O. Box 1028
> Medford OR 97501
> Phone: 800-292-4769
> Fax: 800-242-0329

If you buy potted roses from a local supply house, they are often either from Edmunds or from Jackson and Perkins. The potted roses are not treated very well, have crowded roots, get too cold or hot, too dry or wet, and therefore start out stressed. They are good to buy for $1 each at the end of the selling season, but otherwise should be avoided. I love to buy the $1 specials and grow the unusual varieties which are not popular but may have special characteristics.

People persist in buying bargain roses from the local gas station or anyone else with some space, ignore the basic design of the rose, and then

Here, I grew it myself!

sigh, "Roses are so difficult to grow." Many potted roses at discount stores are covered with wax to keep them from drying out from the neglect they receive at the hands of illiterate clerks, who would rather discuss the latest recording by Snoop Doggie Dog than water their tender charges. The wax covered roses are not the best varieties but off brands like Misthaufen and Water Buffalo. They are so stressed and weak that they make the potted roses at the garden shop look like Jack's beanstalk in comparison.

People who love roses buy only bare root roses, either from the top two suppliers, or from specialty firms (miniature roses, standard roses, old roses). Bare root roses come packed in wet material to keep them alive but fairly dormant. I unpack mine when they arrive and soak them in water, up to 24 hours, to give them a good start when planted.

Pruning

Roses deserve plenty of study before buying, planting, and caring for them. Ignorance of their habits will frustrate the beginner, but following some simple advice based on the principles of Creation will make the job much easier. The rules for growing roses are found in John 15:1-8, even though the lesson is about a grape vine:

> I am the true vine, and my Father is the husbandman. {2} Every branch in me that beareth not fruit he taketh away: and every branch that beareth fruit, he purgeth it, that it may bring forth more fruit. {3} Now ye are clean through the word which I have spoken unto you. {4} Abide in me, and I in you. As the branch cannot bear fruit of itself, except it abide in the vine; no more can ye, except ye abide in me. {5} I am the vine, ye are the branches: He that abideth in me, and I in him, the same bringeth forth much fruit: for without me ye can do nothing. {6} If a man abide not in me, he is cast forth as a branch, and is withered; and men gather them, and cast them into the fire, and they are burned. {7} If ye abide in me, and my words abide in you, ye shall ask what ye will, and it shall be done unto you. {8} Herein is my Father glorified, that ye bear much fruit; so shall ye be my disciples. (John 15:1-8)

Roses grow the way grape vines do, and Christians bear fruit just as grape vines and roses bear fruit.

Roses need to be pruned for two purposes, both good for the plant. If a rose has a branch which is dead wood, the very presence of that branch will sap the strength of the bush and slow down its growth. The unproductive branch, which looks and snaps off like a dead twig, must be pruned away. Pruning makes a rose want to grow. Pruning dead wood takes place all summer, until fall, when pruning would produce tender growth harmed by winter frost. The pruned branches, because they can harbor disease and pests, are thrown away, not allowed to rot under the bush. In the parable of the Vine, Jesus teaches us that we will be removed from the Kingdom if we become dead wood.

The second type of pruning is seldom accepted by novices or practiced. When a rose has bloomed, it must be pruned away when the flower fades. The fading is God's pre-ordained method of setting seed for future roses. Energy is used by the rose to create the seed, and the rose will think its job is done when the first blooms have made their seeds. Cutting the blooms just above five-leaf clusters will force the bush into making more flowers.

Beautiful Flowers, Easy To Grow

Faithful Christians are also pruned in two ways. They are cleansed by the Word of absolution when their sins are forgiven through the power of the Gospel. They are also pruned when they undergo hardships which purify their faith and turn their hearts toward spiritual wisdom from the Scriptures. The pruning of forgiveness makes us fruitful because we no longer carry the burden of sin and we rejoice in the promise of eternal life, knowing Satan is defeated by the cross of Christ. The pruning of affliction makes us fruitful by showing how little the world is concerned with what God loves and how little God is concerned with what loves the world. But we cannot be fruitful apart from the true Vine, Who is Christ. We cannot make ourselves fruitful apart from Him, and all blessings come from Him through the Word, to us and others, not from us to Him.

My sister-in-law complained that her two large roses bushes were not blooming. I offered to doctor the bushes while she went shopping with my wife. When they returned, two-thirds of each bush was pruned away and in the garbage can. Her grateful response was to burst into tears. I said, "Read John 15:1-8. The dead wood must be pruned away. In two weeks you will be thrilled. But you must follow the rest of the lesson. The blooms must be pruned. And remember, these are roses, not cactus plants. They need one bucket of water per bush per week."

Two weeks later the phone rang. "Gregg! You should see the roses. They are completely covered with blooms! They are absolutely gorgeous. I cried when I saw what you did, but now I see they needed it." She began to prune the blooms when they started to fade, mulched the plants with grass clippings, and watered them.

When I visited Larry Carlson, who has lived with ALS (Lou Gehrig's Disease), we discussed pruning experiences. He agreed that he had been pruned a lot and made more fruitful because of it. Lying in bed, completely dependent on a machine for breathing and a tube for feeding, Larry spends his time helping others with ALS. Although healthy people are seldom thankful for their health, Larry is always expressing thanks to God for every blessing. He uses a computer and a special headset to send letters all over the world, to advise people on ALS care, and to organize his fishing trips. His wife Doris goes everywhere to help patients and families with ALS.

When I recently visited a 90 year old member of Faith in New Ulm, her nurse mentioned her own mother dying of ALS. I said, "Have you ever heard of Larry Carlson?" The nurse said, "I know him personally." I soon discovered that her mother was the woman mentioned in the chapter about Larry in *Angel Joy*. So God draws us all together in our pruning experiences, in a global garden rather than village, where we are fruitful if we abide in the Word of Christ.

Planting

Pruning is more important than planting the rose, because pruning is absolutely essential for a summer of flowers. Digging a proper hole is also necessary, because the rose can enjoy all the advantages of Creation principles, with a little foresight. The rose is a heavy feeder because of its habit of growing and blooming when pruned and watered properly. A heavy feeder needs plenty of nitrogen and organic material to keep production going. Sunlight provides most of the energy, but the rose will deplete nitrogen in the soil from blooming and growing new solar collectors (leaves).

Rose roots will reach out in all directions, so they need to be in the best soil possible. Tree roots will effectively throttle the roses by grabbing water and nutrition, so do not plant roses in this competitive environment. If the soil is sandy, compost and old manure can be added to help the area retain water and support a population of earthworms. If the soil is clay, the same amendments will lighten it and make it porous by providing motivation for earthworms to tunnel. An area could be prepared by dumping several inches of organic material on the location in the fall. Or the bad soil could be dug out and replaced in the spring.

The hole should be as large as possible, no smaller than a bushel basket. I have seen roses grow and bloom in dreadful soil, as long as they were watered and pruned. But roses in the best soil will be able to live up to their God-given genetic code. They will resist disease and pests much better when grown in the best soil and mulched to preserve water.

Roses do not like competition, so they should be no closer than three feet apart, to give their roots room to spread and to allow air to circulate. They can have either garlic or chives as companion plants, but they should not have to compete with other vigorous plants. Roses are so distinctive that other plants will clash with them.

Exposure to sunlight is a major consideration in planning where to plant roses. They like plenty of sunlight, but they do not like to be roasted to death, such as growing against a south facing brick wall, which absorbs solar heat and stays hot until midnight. The east or west side of a home may be better in a hotter, sunnier climate, but the south side may be best in the northern regions. The placement of trees and other plants will make a difference. Roses should be where they will thrive and inspire people.

Planting the rose, is fairly easy. The roses should first be soaked in a large container (trash barrel, for instance) with the water covering only their roots. The upper part of the plant would get too soft if submerged. Care should be taken to keep the roots in water most of the time, to prevent air from being taken up and blocking the roots.

When each rose has been planted, the hole should have a teepee of soil in the bottom, so that the roots can be fanned out. If some roots are too long, they can be pruned, which will promote growth in the remaining roots. Soil is added on top of the roots and the bud union is somewhat below the level of the yard in cold areas. Water is added to move the soil around the roots and remove air pockets. The soil is often mounded up around the bush at first, to give the rose a chance to harden up. Later the soil around the rose is made into a dish to catch and hold water when necessary. Clay holds water too well, and sandy soil lets it flow through too fast.

The soil nearest the rose will be the source of blooms for years to come. My mother did not care for the soil in St. Louis and removed it, replacing it with potting soil from the garden center. She pruned and watered according to my instructions and grew awesome roses which threw her neighbor into a coretous fit. His roses were not as grand, and he wanted

Hey, this is my condo!

to know her special secret. Her only secret was using the best soil she could get, pruning, and watering.

Mulching and Watering

God made roses to grow, so they must have food and water. Several inches of grass clippings around the roses will halt weed growth, hold in water, and feed nitrogen to the roses through the earthworms. Some weeds will be introduced by the mulch, but mulch will keep most weeds from taking hold or from getting strong. One rose grower suggests a thick layer of wood mulch, which will help prevent soil borne disease, especially blackspot.

One weed to watch out for is bindweed, since it defies mulch and covertly winds its way up the rose, blooming with cute little morning glory flowers (same family) and producing seed promiscuously. Weeds climb for the sun, so their habit may be used against them by finding the bottom of their stem and pulling out the roots everywhere possible.

Roses demand a lot of water. The rule, worth repeating, is a bucket of water per week per bush. Dripper hoses are good for providing water without wasting a lot. It is also possible to bury a gallon milk jug near the rose bush, after putting some nail holes in the sides. Water and nutrition can be added directly to the roots without a lot of runoff.

Feeding

Roses can be fed on their foliage and through their roots. Grass mulch will feed them, but gardeners may want to add rose food supplements as well. It is better to use too little fertilizer than too much, because a heavy concentration will dry up the rose and kill it, as many have done. My uncle Don put a double dose on the roses and dried them up as effectively as pouring road salt on them.

Some gardeners brew manure and compost tea by adding those ingredients to water and letting them ferment for a few days. This will let chlorine gas evaporate out of the water and give micro-organisms a chance to multiply. (Mosquitoes will love it and should not be given a chance to breed. Linseed oil can be placed on the surface to thwart them.) The idea of compost and manure tea is to take nutrition down into the soil and to crank up the microbial process which can be higher or lower in soil, depending on its organic content.

I have to confess that I have not fed roses, except to put mulch and old manure on the top of the soil. Manure and compost tea are too complicated for me, but may be fun when I have nothing else in the garden to do and no book left to read.

Roses to Buy

People are bewildered by the roses offered in catalogs. They all look breathtaking, and they are. Roses are so attractive that one can offer a single rose in a vase as a gift. Imagine handing someone a single daffodil in a vase, or a dozen daisies! A rose bud will slowly unfold, and if blessed with perfume, scent the room beautified by it.

Roses are inexpensive to grow when we consider that a bush now costs about $10 and yields many blooms, while a single rose at a convenience store will cost around $5. Those who must explain the purchase of 10 rose bushes to a spouse may want to point this out. (I have.) An average rose bush will give us 15-20 blooms, while a heavy producer such as Fragrant Cloud will do even better. The mathematical advantages are compelling.

A group of evergreen bushes in front of the house will elicit no comment. Nor will deciduous bushes. But if the walkway to the home is planted with roses, people will notice and appreciate them. Pruning them will not be much more trouble than pruning other bushes, which yield only scraps. When we prune roses, we have enough blooms to keep vases in the house and plenty for gifts. I usually take roses with me when visiting the hospital or shut-ins. No one has ever objected.

Some popular varieties of roses are listed below and described, to help people make a decision. It is best to buy 3 roses of a type at the same time, for a better effect in the yard and more blooms of the same type, but all roses look good. Their colors clash well together.

Olympiad

Olympiad is the best red rose because of its perfectly shaped bud and the purity of the color, which does not shift toward blue as its matures. When I gave one to our organist, she said later, "The bud was gorgeous, but it became even more beautiful as it opened. I thought I was looking at a painting. I almost cried." Olympiad resists mildew, which is good for those who have excessive rain.

Double Delight

Double Delight is named for its stunning colors and strong perfume. I gave up on it in Columbus, because Japanese beetles simply devoured the blossoms, favoring them over all other roses. My mother has had great success with Double Delight in St. Louis. The flowers are creamy white with strawberry pink edges. Heat makes the pink more intense. It has to be ordered in the fall or winter, or supplies will be gone.

Peace

Peace continues to be a favorite for many reasons, perfume not being on the list. The foliage is unusually attractive and the yellow blooms are especially large. The blooms are tinged with pink as they mature, a softer pink than Double Delight. It can get blackspot, which is the bane of all descendants of the Persian yellow rose, but it outgrows the blackspot. Peace can only be criticized for being stingy with its blooms.

Fragrant Cloud

Fragrant Cloud produces a rose which is sometimes called deep orange, coral red, or brick. Climate affects both color and fragrance. The bloom is exceptionally large and overflowing with perfume. One bud will scent a room. I planted my first one near a rain downspout and credited that with the high production of blooms. Later I learned that Fragrant Cloud is famous for abundant blooms, resistance to disease, and ability to survive winter.

Queen Elizabeth, the Creation Rose

Queen Elizabeth is a large bush, able to reach 9 feet tall, a grandiflora, developed by an orthodox Lutheran, Walter Lamments, Ph. D., who professed his faith in Creation and argued against evolution. The blooms are a delicate salmon pink. Some call Queen Elizabeth the greatest rose of all. Harsh pruning creates a spectacular show of blooms. This rose is as simple to grow as Fragrant Cloud but its size must be considered when planting. I planted one on each side of the front porch in Columbus, and they stood as tall as most evergreen bushes. If they had been planted beside other roses, they would have looked like cretins.

Tropicana

The opposite in size to Queen Elizabeth is Tropicana, known for the brightness of its red-orange blooms and their ability to last as cut flowers. The fragrance is considered "fruity." The advantage of Tropicana is that they can be squeezed into a space which would be too small for some other roses.

Big Purple

I had fun with Big Purple in Columbus. The blooms are not only big and purple, as one might expect, but perfumed as well. Fragrance was almost forgotten in rose breeding, but now it is coming back.

Europeana

Europeana belongs to the class of roses called floribunda for their prolific blooms. Floribundas should be planted to take advantage of their mass of color, used as a hedge. Europeana is prone to mildew, but it is still considered one of the best roses and has attractive foliage.

Climbers

Climbing roses will require more attention and fussing, so they should be considered if they are appropriate for the situation. I would rather send a rambler up a tree or across the ground than coax a climbing rose into the right kind of growth.

Tree Roses

Tree roses, properly called standard roses, are the elite of all roses. The typical hybrid rose is grafted onto a wild rose root, to make it more resistant to winter. A tree rose goes another step by having a long woody stem (a standard) grafted between the hybrid rose and the wild rose root. Two bud union grafts on the standard rose make it more vulnerable to frost and more expensive to buy.

The rarity of tree roses makes them attractive to those who want to showboat for the neighbors. They need to be staked, and they need to be buried in the winter to preserve the standard and upper bud union. My wife's parents like tree roses because they were considered so special in Hungary, where they were born. Sometimes Jackson and Perkins will have leftover standard roses and offer them for a very low price, closer to the price of a hybrid tea rose.

Simplicity

Many more kinds of roses are being sold today: antique, English, rugosa, and miniature. One rose which is wildly popular is Simplicity, by Jackson and Perkins. It comes in white, red, and pink. The bloom does not have the form of a hybrid tea, but the plant is completely trouble free, resistant to all pests and diseases, and does not require pruning. I found a gardener in Columbus who figured out that it was cheaper to plant Simplicity than to build a fence, so he ordered 200 plants and rented a post hole digger. Later that summer his corner lot was fenced with a mass of pink blooms. I used Simplicity to fence off the end of the church parking lot in Columbus. The soil was the gravel base of the asphalt lot and I ran out of time to replace it. I dug holes, dropped in Simplicity, and watered. They bloomed with abandon.

Pests and Diseases

Roses do attract more insect pests than most flowers, but only two insects are really destructive.

The aphid loves to suck out the juices of the bud before it opens, ruining the blossom. Aphids can be knocked off the bud or sprayed away with water. Garlic and soap solutions can also be used to repel them.

The other destructive rose pest is the fat, obnoxious, piggish Japanese beetle. These gluttons not only devour roses blooms, but also fly into the face of anyone who disturbs their habitat. Their numbers can be reduced with traps and with milky spore disease. The traps use an aroma which makes the beetles "romantic," so they climb into a paper sack and stay there. Milky spore disease is a fungus from Japan which will turn their grubs' blood milky in the soil where they live, making them explode and spreading the spore. The treatment for the soil is expensive and slow, and does not prevent beetles from flying in from another location.

The worse disease is blackspot, a fungus from the soil which starts on the bottom leaf of the plant and works up. The leaves slowly die and fall off, spreading the disease. Every blackspot leaf must be removed early and thrown away; the leaf will die anyway, once infected. The loss of leaves will reduce the solar-collecting energy of the rose. The best way to prevent blackspot is to avoid roses which succumb to blackspot, such as the yellow rose Oregold. A thick wood mulch will keep the blackspot spores from coming up from the soil. Removing infected leaves is important, but having a strong, well fed, pruned rose will help most of all. Disease and insects kill weak plants but leave strong ones alone.

Another common problem, which has never been serious for me, is mildew. Damp weather will promote mildew, but some roses are resistant while others are vulnerable. Plenty of space will help the roses dry out.

Winter Protection

The best winter protection is a thick blanket of snow. When four feet of snow covered the ground all winter in Michigan, hardly any roses died. A sub-zero spell with little snow will penetrate the plants and freeze them dead. Winter protection begins with mounding up soil or compost around each rose, forming a teepee of soil, about a bushel basket full. Leaves or bags of leaves can be added on top of the soil to give more protection. The more cautious will dig a trench and heel the plant over into the soil for the winter. Tree roses must be buried in this fashion to survive.

Winter protection also requires the discipline of not pruning or picking roses late in the fall. They are often at their best at this time, but it is better to let them set seed and go dormant for the winter rather than to wake them up and force new growth in time for a harsh freeze.

Spring Pruning

Some rosarians advocate pruning in the dead of winter. Most wait until spring, when the first growth begins to show itself. At that time I cut off all dead wood, no matter where it is. (John 15:1-8) I also cut away branches which fill the center or cross, to give the bush the shape of a vase. I am inclined to prune more harshly, removing about half of its growth. This not only helps wake up the bush to make it more fruitful, but also motivates the roots to grow. Some will chop through the soil to prune the roots a little, to encourage them. That would be done away from the base, so the main roots remain whole. The generative power of the rose is impressive, as long as it receives enough water and food.

The first blooms will arrive in May and June, depending on weather and climate. A bud may be cut when the five sepals around it are open. Then the bud will slowly turn into a flower in a vase. The stem may be as long as necessary, but the cut should be above a five-leaf cluster on the branch. That will encourage quick growth of more buds. Haphazard cutting and pruning will not promote bud formation as easily. Some people will slant the cut and paint over the cut with a special solution. Do I have time to paint rose branches?

Fun with Roses

Children are fascinated with roses and enjoy hearing about God's Creation. In Columbus, they always came over to get roses for their mothers. They were given roses only if they could name the kind they wanted. Asking for a yellow or red one was futile. They quickly learned to ask for Oregold, Queen Elizabeth, or Olympiad by name. They knew that Fragrant Cloud had the most perfume and Oregold the most blackspot. From time to time, we discussed how God created plants and animals each with a special purpose.

Some of the girls kept every bloom to build up a rose potpourri. When rose petals are dried, whether the variety is perfumed or not, they will give off a perfume for a long time. The best way to store them at first is a wicker basket, where they will have plenty of air while drying and not get moldy. They shrink, so it takes quite a few petals. When the petals are completely dry, they can be put in a cloth bag and hung in the closet or used in the dresser.

Rose clippings can be placed in a glass of water, where they will root. Given enough care, they can turn into a rose bush, although this is frowned upon by the people who spent years developing the variety. Their patent prevents people from xeroxing rose plants for free. However, it may be done by roses in the public domain.

NOTES

C. F. W. Walther, *The Proper Distinction between Law and Gospel*, St. Louis: Concordia Publishing House, 1928, p. 21.

FIVE

Good Food and Good Nutrition, for Almost No Cost

 ardening with the principles of Creation in mind will yield fabulous flowers which delight the senses, whether the blooms come from bulbs, roses, annuals or perennials. When the same principles are applied to raising vegetables, herbs, and salad greens, the beauty of the garden is enhanced by the improved health of the whole family.

We often see pictures of starving people living on parched land and wonder, "How can they survive on so little?" Then we turn our attention to manufactured snacks of dubious quality and no nutritional value. Much of our food is processed to include a maximum amount of these food groups: starch, salt, sugar, and grease.

If we return to the concept of God designing all plants and animals for a purpose, then the food we grow will have maximum nutrition, excellent taste, and cost us very little. We will be no healthier than the soil in which we grow our food. So we plant with thanksgiving, knowing how little we do for the harvest and how much is done by the Creator:

We plow the fields and scatter the good seed on the land,
But it is fed and watered by God's almighty hand. He sends the
snow in winter, the warmth to swell the grain,
The breezes and the sunshine, and soft refreshing rain.
　　　Refrain:　　　All good gifts around us are sent from
　　　　　　　　　heaven above,
　　　　　　　　　Then thank the Lord, oh, thank the Lord,

for all His love.

He only is the maker of all things near and far;
He paints the wayside flower,
He lights the evening star.
The wind and waves obey Him; by Him the birds are fed.
Much more to us, His children, He gives us daily bread.[24]

Gardening draws us closer to Creation by showing us how foolish we are and how great is the wisdom and power of the Lord.

Bless the LORD, O my soul. O LORD my God, thou art very great; thou art clothed with honour and majesty. {2} Who coverest thyself with light as with a garment: who stretchest out the heavens like a curtain: {3} Who layeth the beams of his chambers in the waters: who maketh the clouds his chariot: who walketh upon the wings of the wind: {4} Who maketh his angels spirits; his ministers a flaming fire: {5} Who laid the foundations of the earth, that it should not be removed for ever. (Psalm 104:1-5)

The application of the spiritual wisdom which comes from the Word of God is apparent:

He sendeth the springs into the valleys, which run among the hills. {11} They give drink to every beast of the field: the wild asses quench their thirst. {12} By them shall the fowls of the heaven have their habitation, which sing among the branches. {13} He watereth the hills from his chambers: the earth is satisfied with the fruit of thy works. {14} He causeth the grass to grow for the cattle, and herb for the service of man: that he may bring forth food out of the earth; {15} And wine that maketh glad the heart of man, and oil to make his face to shine, and bread which strengtheneth man's heart. {16} The trees of the LORD are full of sap; the cedars of Lebanon, which he hath planted; {17} Where the birds make their nests: as for the stork, the fir trees are her house. {18} The high hills are a refuge for the wild goats; and the rocks for the conies. {19} He appointed the moon for seasons: the sun knoweth his going down. {20} Thou makest darkness, and it is night: wherein all the beasts of the forest do creep forth. {21} The young lions roar after their prey, and seek their meat from God. {22} The sun ariseth, they gather themselves together, and lay them down in their dens. {23} Man goeth forth unto his work and to his labour until the evening. {24} O LORD, how manifold are thy works! in wisdom hast thou made them all: the earth is full of thy riches. (Psalm 104:10-24)

Whether we know it or not, whether we believe it or not, these things are true and will remain true until the end of time, even if no one is left on earth who can say, "I believe in God the Father Almighty, Maker of heaven and earth..."[25]

When inorganic theories of agriculture took over, during the Babylonian Captivity of the Soil, the topsoil was depleted and exploited until it blew away in the Dust Bowl of the 1930s. Those who lived through those times remember not being able to escape the dirt which blew into homes and hung in the air. The sun was often blotted out in a man-made plague of darkness, caused by violating the laws of Creation.

In contrast, *Organic Gardening* magazine and the books of Rodale Press have shown that nightmarish soil can be turned into a paradise by adding enough organic material and letting God's appointed servants turn manure and vegetable trash into light, fertile soil. Research has shown that the produce grown on land with a high earthworm population, that is, soil with a rich supply of humus, will have more vitamins and minerals than produce grown on depleted soil.

Jerry Minnich, author of *The Earthworm Book*, has gathered information on *Gardening for Maximum Nutrition*, from various studies. Organically grown kale had 93 percent more vitamin C. Spinach had 89% more vitamin C.[26] Brussels sprouts, kohlrabi, and endive all had more vitamin C. It seems reasonable that a blend of ingredients in the compost will enhance the vitamin and mineral content of the plants which benefit from it.

Therefore, favoring the earthworm will also favor the health of the family by adding vitamins and minerals to everyone's diet. Freshness will naturally increase the amount of nutrition in the produce, since some vitamins do not last well in shipping. Freshness will also make many untouchable vegetables appealing. It may be that gardeners are really gourmands who want to work and eat at the same time. Their children will find out that many vegetables which are "good for you" on the dinner table are just plain delicious after a chase through the yard, a game of baseball, or a bike ride.

Three considerations in planning the vegetable and herb garden are:
1) Will it be fairly easy to grow?

2) Does the food value and the taste make it worth growing?
3) Will it save us money?

Some foods are so easy to grow that they require no care. For instance, lettuce can be sown like grass seed. Some foods are worth growing for their flavor when fresh, since they change when they are picked. Peas and corn turn their sugar into starch as soon as they are picked, so growing them will forever reduce one's desire to buy peas and corn at the store or along the highway.

A few vegetables may seem to be a lot of trouble, but that is why they cost so much at the store. Asparagus requires more initial effort and time, but the return is worth it when fresh store asparagus is $1.50 a pound, frozen asparagus is limp, and canned asparagus is an abomination.

Cold Tolerant Vegetables

Gardeners waste a lot of time waiting for weather which is good for one type of plant but bad for another. God has designed a number of common vegetables to grow in cold weather. They actually manufacture their own anti-freeze. While an egg plant will crumple from the first light frost, kale can be picked fresh in the snow on New Year's Day.

Some vegetables prefer cold weather and sometimes need frost to reach their peak of flavor. Those who garden in colder states have an advantage, since they can modify the climate with certain gadgets to guard against frost. In Columbus, Ohio, work during the day was limited by a wind chill of 120 degrees Fahrenheit. Work in the cooler twilight was prevented by hordes of mosquitoes, maddened by their inability to reach the humans who hid indoors.

Spinach

Spinach is one of the best vegetables to grow, since fresh spinach in the store is rubbery at best. The mere thought of canned spinach is an appetite suppressant. Spinach is best in cool weather when full of water, which makes it crunchy. Heat makes it go to seed (bolt), a process which can be slowed down by lopping off the seed heads, but not prevented. We eat the leaves, not the seeds, so the formation of seeds marks the end of the plant as food.

One fall I followed the suggestion found in a magazine and planted spinach in Michigan for the following spring. I planted it early enough so that the plants would just emerge from the ground. The hard frosts were coming, so I covered the plants with autumn leaves. As soon as the snow was off the ground, I uncovered the spinach plants, which were still green. They grew well in the cold spring rains and laughed at insects, which were still in the larva stage or too cold to come from their shelter. I was harvesting perfect, insect free spinach before others had planted theirs.

Spinach is noted for being high in vitamin A and calcium, with modest amounts of iron, riboflavin, and vitamin C.

Three Planting Secrets

Those who advocate higher production in the garden have abandoned the idea of creating neat narrow rows of vegetables, as if plants need to

line up like soldiers in parade. Rows keep plants from forming their own leaf mulch and waste a lot of space. I see a lot of gardens where the bare rows encourage weed growth and soil erosion.   I loosen up an area for spinach with a metal rake, sprinkle seed in the loose soil, and tamp it down with a metal hoe. Spinach is more of a grass, so I grow spinach in patches rather than in platoons, brigades, and divisions. I often mulch the emerging seedlings with grass clippings or leaves, but not enough to block the sunlight from them.

Germinating seeds need a steady supply of water. The roots are just forming, so they grow at a phenomenal rate at first. Gardeners have seed germination problems because they think seed in soil will grow, so their surviving plants do seem to be expensive and difficult to grow. If the soil is not damp to the touch, the newly planted seeds are drying up rather than growing.

People will naturally hope that it rains steadily after planting. The secret to that is planting after a full moon, since a full moon is almost always accompanied by a high pressure zone, cooler nights, and a cloudless sky. A full moon is also an indication of frost, since clouds serve as blankets to hold down the heat radiating from the ground. Rain is more likely after a full moon, so pay attention to that old wives' tale.

Lettuce

Lettuce wilts in the heat and loves cool weather, but it goes to seed due to the length of days, while spinach bolts from heat. The neighbor's security light will have an affect on lettuce bolting early.

Lettuce can also be sown like grass seed, early in the season, before most seeds will germinate or survive. Some early crops of lettuce can be obtained from sowing lettuce where flowers will be planted later. This led to the following exchange:

"Pastor, is that lettuce growing in the planter in front of the parsonage?"

"Yes it is. Why?"

"I told my wife I saw lettuce in the planter, and she said I was crazy."

"The lettuce will be done before I put in marigold plants. It is very cold tolerant."

"Oh."

Lettuce does not offer a lot of nutrition, but it remains a popular plant for the garden. Many types of leaf lettuce can be grown. I was surprised to find my French horticultural lettuce waving in the garden when no breeze could be felt. Walking closer, I saw a baby rabbit enjoying a leaf, tearing away a little at a time. He was not very wary, so I walked up very close and watched him. His home was probably nearby, but I did not want to disturb him or his siblings. His parents were obviously enjoying the garden, too, but I had so much I never noticed any damage.

Lettuce offers some iron, calcium, and vitamin A.

Peas

Peas are like spinach, hardy enough to be planted in the fall and harvested in the spring. One gardener drilled holes in the frozen ground to plant them in the spring. I always started them as early as possible (February in Michigan) knowing they would conk out in the warmer weather. One time my seeds were covered with several inches of snow. Members of the church said, "Oh no."

I said, "They are snow peas, aren't they?" And they did very well, insulated and watered by the snow.

Peas have shallow roots and love sweet soil. They can be soaked in water for 24 hours, to help them germinate faster. Fireplace ashes would be a good amendment for the pea patch, to sweeten the soil. The tendrils need support, so it is good to fasten chicken wire to a wall or between poles for support. The same area can be used for beans later in the season, when peas are done.

Seeds are fairly inexpensive, especially when bought in large quantities from the suppliers rather than in tiny pouches at the store. Local seed suppliers will often have bulk seeds, which led to this conversation at the store.

"I need some edible pod peas."

"How much."

"Two pounds."

"Two pounds!"

"They are my second planting."

"Second planting?"

"I already planted a pound a month ago."

By planting large quantities early I was able to get a huge crop which fed us and all our friends to the point of complete satiety. Rabbits love pea vines as they emerge from the ground, but we never lost the crop in Michigan. In some areas, like Ohio, where everyone has a deck and a warren of rabbits under the deck, peas will not survive the predation.

I favor edible pod peas, which can be eaten pod and all. They can also be allowed to mature and shelled for the peas alone. Traditional peas need to be shelled.

Peas are very high in thiamin and niacin, containing iron, riboflavin, and vitamin C.

More Fruit, Not a Secret

Peas and beans are like roses and grapes: they are more fruitful if pruned after fruiting. (John 15:1-8) The vine first flowers, then tries to form seeds after being pollinated. If the peas and beans are harvested steadily, the plants will continue to flower and form pods. If left alone, the vines will harden up the pods and quit producing.

We had members in the church in Midland who were from Hong Kong. They told us about a special Oriental delicacy called "dragons' claws," made from the tendrils. Pea vines were grown for the upper tendrils alone, which sold at an astronomical price. We knew that cutting the tendrils would only promote growth, so we invited them over and harvested shopping bags of "dragons' claws." They were staggered at the value of the tendrils in Hong Kong terms and said, "Are you sure? Do you know what they are worth? No one ever has so much in Hong Kong." The pea vines grew even better and produced more after being declawed.

Pea vines are high in nitrogen, so they make great additions to the compost pile. They can also be fed to pet rabbits, who will enjoy the treat while adding nitrogen and bacteria to the compost.

Kale

Kale belongs to the cabbage (brassica) family, offering a lot of nutrition and the hardiness of a polar bear. Kale not only tolerates frost but loves it. Ornamental kale, which is often planted for a mass of color near office buildings, is just as edible as ordinary kale, so it can serve as a colorful border as well as food for the winter. Cold is said to improve its flavor.

Kale seeds can be started indoors about a month before the last frost, or seedings can be purchased and planted after the last frost. The plants require little care. Mulch will keep them fed and hold water in the soil.

We kept our kale growing in Michigan until New Year's Day. I went out into the snow, groped around, and harvested kale which was fresh and green. Someone will wonder, "Loaded with vitamins. Stays green in the snow. What is the downside?" Kale is favored in corporate landscaping and around salad bars because it is a little less tender than plastic.

Kale deserves to be grown for fun and as a small part of the diet. It can be chopped up and blended with other salads, or cooked. Kale is very high in calcium and vitamin C, containing vitamin A, riboflavin and niacin as well.

Cabbage

Cabbage is another nutritious member of the brassica family. They are planted the same as kale, either directly in the soil as seeds, or as seedlings after the first frost, to give them an earlier start.

Cabbages are easy to grow. Slugs and cabbage moths like them. Slugs can be minimized by trapping and by surrounding plants with diatomaceous earth, which will slice up and kill errant slugs. Cabbage moths lay eggs which hatch into caterpillars which are preyed upon by wasps. It is fun to watch wasps prowling in the brassica plants, looking for someone to devour.

Cabbages can be harvested whenever they seem large enough to pick, a definite advantage for those who want to pick them fresh over a period of time. They are somewhat high in vitamin C.

Brussels Sprouts

Brussels sprouts form a spike on which little cabbage heads form. They are sweeter after a frost and very resistant to the cabbage worm. The seeds will tolerate going into the soil two months before the last frost. Seedlings are often available at garden centers. They like rich soil, as do their cousins, the cabbages.

Brussels sprouts are fairly high in vitamin C and contain niacin and riboflavin as well. They are harvested from the bottom of the plant, where they mature first. The plant will continue to produce more sprouts, even after frost has wiped out the garden.

Broccoli

The nutritional superstar of the brassica family is broccoli, with very high amounts of riboflavin and vitamin C, plenty of calcium, plus niacin, vitamin A, potassium, protein, and some iron.

We eat broccoli buds, which will grow again when harvested. If left alone too long, the buds will flower with the yellow bloom characteristic of its family. The whole family is aromatic, so to speak, when cooked, and a mainstay for nutrition.

If someone is going to grow just one brassica, then broccoli should be the choice, based on ease of growing and nutrition. In contrast, another family member, cauliflower, is touchy about budding and much lower in nutrition. Cauliflower is eaten raw as a snack, like broccoli. Cooked cauliflower is a lot like egg plant, good when combined with something else which has flavor.

Collards

This brassica is grown for its leaves, which are loaded with calcium, vitamin A and C, with thiamine, riboflavin, and niacin in lower amounts. The leaves are cooked or eaten raw when combined with other salad greens.

Collards are easy to grow. Like many leafy plants, the leaves can be harvested over a period of time, the youngest leaves being the most tender. One of the joys of gardening is thinning spinach, carrots, collards, beets, and radishes, enjoying the most succulent plants.

Dandelions

There is little need to advise people on how to grow dandelions, the most popular herb in America, giving employment to thousands in a vain attempt to wipe them out through broad leaf weed killers. Dandelion greens are extremely high in calcium and vitamin A, containing some iron, thiamine, and riboflavin as well.

Gourmet salad growers swear that early spring dandelion greens are delicious. They tend to be bitter soon after. They should be harvested only where they are free of herbicide and pesticide. American Indians called them "lawn nails," due to their ability to resist being pulled up. In a pesticide and herbicide free yard, some dandelions can be left to grow. A highly organic soil will probably also produce the goosefoot weed, which is edible and high in nutrition. Goosefoot is easy to identify, since the leaf looks exactly like a goose's foot. Goosefoot leaves are never bitter, unlike dandelions, which get bitter as the season progresses.

Some people buy dandelion seeds and raise them as a crop. The only problem is that the dandelion patch can get infested with grass.

Asparagus

Many people have picked wild asparagus in the country, growing along fences where birds have roosted. The usual excuse for not growing asparagus is simply that "It takes too long." One person admitted not growing asparagus for 10 years because of the delay in harvesting the first crop.

Asparagus is frightfully expensive and good: all the more reason to grow it. The nutritional value is slight, but it is good raw and extraordinary when cooked correctly.

Asparagus has an extensive system of roots which store energy to produce the sprouts which we enjoy so much. Left alone, the sprouts will turn into ferns which send energy to the roots and produce seed. My wife's uncle bought a home and plowed under an asparagus patch because he did not connect the exotic ferns with the delicious spears. He was amazed at the wormy root system which defies description. Too late, he realized that he took out asparagus and never replanted it. "It takes too long."

Asparagus roots grow sideways and are extensive, so a good patch will be dug out first with the soil amended or replaced by compost and old manure. Because the roots go sideways, the compost and manure trench should be wide rather than deep. All kinds of strange and mystical instructions may be followed in planting the crowns, which are purchased from a supplier, but God grows them when sown from a fence.

The crowns look like tiny mop heads made out of cork, not really alive. If they are covered with soil, they will grow. Some suppliers sell "male only" asparagus, to prevent energy from going into seed production. The key to having a good patch of asparagus is giving them time to get entrenched with energy built up in the root system. That means letting them fern out for the first two years. No spears are cut for the first two years. Then only the spears as big as a man's thumb are cut. Asparagus harvested from the garden will be much more tender and juicy than store asparagus, and the home gardener does not need to harvest so much of the lower part, which is woodier.

Asparagus needs plenty of room to grow, as much as two feet between crowns, so tomatoes can sprawl between them. Praying mantis egg cases near the asparagus will keep the asparagus beetle from getting too far in chewing up the ferns.

Some people add salt to the asparagus crop, but that goes against my grain. I try to keep the soil fertile with mulch and with manure when it's available.

Sweet Corn

Once the soil warms up more, it is time to start sweet corn. Corn is getting as complicated as roses. There are now 3 main types:
1) Regular hybrids, such as Silver Queen, a pure white variety.
2) Super sweet hybrids, such as Butterfruit (bi-color), which convert their sugar to starch more slowly after picking. These need warm soil to germinate and must be isolated from other kinds of corn.
3) Sugar enhanced, considered the sweetest and tenderest kind, with better flavor.

At first, only white corn was considered good for people to eat. Yellow corn was for animals. Now yellow and bi-color corn are the most popular.

No one who has eaten corn from the garden, a few minutes after picking, will question whether it deserves a place in the Wormhaven garden. Sweet corn will create friends and warm up neighbors faster than inheriting a billion dollars. Even the undertaker will be sad when a grower of sweet corn dies.

To grow superb corn, one must consider the characteristics of the plant, which God has endowed with so many virtues. First of all, it is a heavy feeder, requiring a lot of organic material in the soil and plenty of nitrogen for growth. My best patch was grown on top of 4 feet of compost, mulched heavily with grass clippings. Corn is very efficient in using the sun's energy (topped only by the sunflower) and must have plenty of sun to grow.

Secondly, corn has an extensive root system. Walking on the soil near corn will damage the roots and slow down the growth of the plant. The corn patch should have a walkway of boards or paving stones to prevent soil compaction.

Thirdly, corn is wind pollinated, so the patch must have plenty of rows (at least 4) to allow the wind to carry the pollen. The corn may be planted farther apart for air circulation, to decrease smut, which is aggravated by dampness. The corn may be planted closer together to increase the yield.

Corn is upright in growth, a glorified grass, so it will serve as a good

companion for low-growing, spreading plants. The classic companion for corn is a pumpkin vine, said to annoy squirrels with its prickly vine while shading the ground. Pumpkins are also heavy feeders, so the combination requires plenty of food and water for success. Abraham Lincoln planted the pumpkins in his father's corn patch, so children can be encouraged to do the same today, with a little lesson in history.

Pole beans can be planted near corn, once the corn is started. They will climb the stalks and feed nitrogen to the corn roots. Children enjoy picking beans pods off the corn, but pumpkin vines will make that unlikely, except for the outside rows.

Corn is ready to pick once the silk is completely brown. Racoons and squirrels know the exact moment. Many gardeners on the edge of civilization have told about the entire patch being raided at night. The only solution is an electric wire fence.

Corn has some niacin, but most people would grow it if it had nothing of value but the flavor. Corn on the cob stirs up memories of picnics, pig roasts, and family reunions.

Bad ears of corn can be stripped and left out for birds to enjoy. The patch can be chopped down and left to rot at the end of the season or put into the compost bin. Corn and pumpkins take a lot out of the soil, but they put even more back in, if the plant is allowed to rot or compost.

Corn has a few problems and pests, but it is best to remember that disease and insects attack weak, malnourished plants which do not get enough water.

Beans

Green beans can be planted in the bush or pole variety. The challenge with bush beans is harvesting them fast enough and finding them all. They are not loaded with nutrition, but they are so easy to grow that most people enjoy having some. We seldom cook them, since Martin and Chris eat them raw. When I want them cooked, they consider it a waste of perfectly good plants.

Beans, peas and vetch are legumes, so they harbor bacteria which transform gaseous nitrogen into nitrogen compounds needed by other plants. Beans and peas are a good rotation crop to use with corn, since corn uses up so much nitrogen in the soil.

The most nutritious beans are navy beans (protein, phosphorous, iron, potassium, iron) and great northern beans, both used as dry beans and cooked.

Pole beans are fun to grow on corn, but they do not like the chemicals sent out by sunflower roots. The bean teepee is great for children. This is how to build one.

1. Find a pole or metal tubing and wedge it into the ground so that the top is about 6 feet tall.
2. Run garden fencing around a perimeter.
3. Fill the inside of the fencing with plenty of grass or spoiled hay, if lawn is being reclaimed.
4. Cultivate the outside of the perimeter for planting pole beans or scarlet runner beans, whose flowers are loved by humming birds. Other exotic beans may be tried, since the teepee tends to show them off well.
5. Run twine from the fence to the top of the pole, but leave an entrance for the children.
6. Watch the beans run up the twine, flower, and fill out. Children love to climb inside and harvest the beans for themselves.
7. In the fall, pull aside the grass or hay floor, and plant crocus and daffodils underneath. They will bloom through the flooring in the spring when it is too cold to use, then fade away in time for another bean crop.

Carrots

Carrots are touchy, but make up for it by being sweet and crammed with vitamin A. Because they are a root crop and start out as tiny seeds, they need soft soil and daily applications of moisture. While most seeds can be planted in a trench dug by a metal hoe, carrots seeds would rather have an area dug up to a depth of one foot. The seed can be sown about one month before the last frost in the area. To get a good crop, water the area every day, unless it rains.

We have all had carrots which are little better than wood. The plant really wants to grow two years, setting seed in the second year, just like its toxic cousin, queen ann's lace, also called wild carrot. If the carrots grow too long, they tend to be a little woody. When they are thinned out, they are tender and succulent. If the soil is free of clay, which clings to root crops, the carrots can be thinned and eaten at the same time. The aromatic greens are good for the compost or the pet rabbits.

Carrots will tolerate frost and tend to get sweeter with some cold. If they are insulated by bales of hay, they can be left in the ground and harvested during the winter. Freezing will make them mushy.

Beets and Swiss Chard

Beets and swiss chard belong to the same family. Their seeds are really pods of seeds. Both plants produce leaves which are used for salad. Swiss chard leaves are a good substitute for spinach during hot weather. Repeated cuttings can be taken during the summer.

Beets are hated or loved as a food. We have a photo of our son Martin as a baby, with bright red beets oozing out of his mouth, a big smile on his face. It is usually necessary to thin beets, since most people will plant them as seeds rather than as pods of seeds. The baby plants are good to eat.

The Nightshades:
Tomatoes, Potatoes, Eggplant

Nightshades should not be grown next to each other. The most popular one to grow is the ornamental berry turned into a vegetable: the tomato. Unless the tomato has been bred for nutrition, it has little to offer (some vitamin C and so forth) but flavor. A restaurant tomato and a store tomato will never compare to a sun-warmed tomato from the garden.

Tomatoes have many virtues which make them welcome in all gardens. They are great for throwing and make a satisfying squish when they hit. This is not a foolish waste of time. No plant will volunteer more freely than a tomato, perhaps exceeding even the often slandered dandelion. A tomato seed will survive almost any kind of abuse and come up the next spring at exactly the right time to produce a fine plant. When a tomato seems too gamey to be eaten, toss it in the garden or throw it against the garage. Its seeds will germinate next spring. If the plant is in the wrong place, transplant it or pull it out. If not, enjoy it.

Tomatoes will produce better when supported. Their fruit is attractive to various insects and the vines flop on the ground without support. The gardener may use cages or tie the vines to twine to give them maximum sun and air.

Tomatoes are fairly sensitive to cold, but nothing like egg plants. Various schemes can be used (such as glass and plastic jugs over them, or the Wall o' Water) to keep them warm and make them fruit a little faster. Green tomatoes can be picked and ripened in the sun on the window sill. Do not take them into the basement and forget them as I did, only to find a mushy mess a month later.

Cherry tomatoes are great for children and adults. They seem to be a little sweeter. It is also easier to eat one without puree of tomato running down the chin and shirt. Cherry tomatoes will run up chicken wire easily enough and will also climb bushes and fruit. And why not? Their cousin, woody nightshade, will climb in the bushes and produce berries galore, finding the spots of sunlight necessary for production. Vines seem attracted to bushes, so the trick is to match them up appropriately.

Tomatoes make a great companion plant to asparagus, favoring both plants and repelling insects to some degree. Tomatoes are traditionally grown with sweet basil as well. Basil smells so good that it is considered a remedy for depression. It is also the herb which goes best with tomatoes in cooking.

Potatoes get no respect, because they are inexpensive to buy, grow in the ground, and have a terrible reputation for making people fat. They are really a vitamin pill in disguise, the most popular vegetable with so many vitamins: plenty of potassium, thiamine, and niacin, with some vitamin C, protein, phosphorous as well.

The potato is really a tuber, but knowing the difference will not affect the garden. The eyes of a potato can be dug into the ground or planted under spoiled hay. Either way, they will grow and spread by turning sunlight into starch and vitamins. They are ready to harvest when the vines start to die back. The Borgia side of the family is manifested by the green spots which grow on the tubers if sunlight falls on them directly. The green spots are toxic and should be cut away. They may be the origin of our association of green with poison, but they are not enough to keep people away from potatoes.

Potatoes are healthy for everyone to eat, but they are too often used as a fat delivery system. Either they are frozen, soaked in shortening, and fried into nutritional zombie-land, or they are baked for a month and loaded with sour cream and a yellow substance called butter. Garden potatoes are so superior to store potatoes that everyone should try growing them. After having fresh, even baby potatoes, from the garden, the thought of a restaurant potato will be disgusting. Potatoes like sunlight and a somewhat acid soil. They are not particular.

Jerusalem artichokes (which are not artichokes or from Jerusalem, but a sunflower) may be grown instead of potatoes or in addition to potatoes. Their tubers are nutritious and not so starchy as potatoes. The tubers will multiply in the soil if not completely harvested, which can be good or bad, depending on the situation.

Eggplants. They fall over dead at the first frost, so they are good indicators of what happened last night. They are like those Job's comforters who stop by after something bad has happened and offer generous counsel about why it was your fault.

Eggplants have been bred to have fruit which look just like eggs. Normally they are a dark purple. The daughter of a friend had her hair died egg plant, so the mother kept explaining and apologizing to everyone. I believe the daughter soon changed her hair color to its original color when boys stopped asking her out. Boys do not like to reminded of egg plants when they see a girl. Egg plants stir up the emotions, not due to their total lack of flavor or nutrition, but because they are loved and hated without reason.

Start up a conversation in a crowded room about egg plants and those people who adore them will immediately start defending them in a way which makes the critic feel uneasy. I grew eggplants as organic thermometers in Michigan and gave the survivors away to our neighbor, who kept saying, "Are you sure you want me to have all these?" She questioned my sanity, so I have concluded that people are irreversibly polarized on the subject of eggplant.

Pumpkins and Squash, Gourds

Gardeners need to know that pumpkins are squash and that most pumpkin pie filling is not from pumpkins but from squash. Learning this has not deterred me from eating pumpkin pie, but encouraged me, since the squash family is known to be fairly high in potassium, riboflavin, vitamin A and C.

Pumpkins are heavy feeders and produce flesh which is fairly rough. The vines threaten the whole yard and need a lot of room. If they were not sensitive to frost, they would cover us up like the kudzu vines which were foolishly imported to America. Pumpkins are grown for carving and to fill in the spaces between corn stalks.

Blue hubbard squash is perfect for large amounts of smooth squash. If space is a problem, they may be bought at a stand rather than grown. The winter squashes all store well, which is part of God's plan. They keep inside for months and can be enjoyed most of the winter. A member of Faith in New Ulm gave us garden squash in January. Butternut and acorn squash are popular but small, and not as smooth as hubbard.

Zucchini squash is a summer squash, lower in nutrition. Many people like zukes in salad or use them to make mock apple pie. One conversation keeps taking place with other gardeners:

"Do you grow zucchinis?"

"Never do."

"I have some extras. Our garden is loaded with them. Don't you like them?"

"We use them all the time."

"But why don't you grow them?"

"Because everyone starts giving them away at this time every year."

Gourds are also cucurbits, with similar leaves and flowers. They come in all sizes and shapes. They are fun to watch as they grow into a bush, flower, fruit, and fade away. The gourds change color and get lighter as they ripen and dry out. They make good ornaments indoors. When our gourds finally started to go bad, I buried them in the compost and soon had gourds marching across the chicken wire on the garage and growing in the bushes. Children like to take them home, let them dry, and shake the dry seeds inside.

Raspberries and Blackberries

Fall is a good time to order and plant two bramble plants: raspberries and blackberries. The roots will grow in the winter, especially if the plant is mulched, giving them a stronger start in the spring. In fact, most bushes and trees will also be better if planted in the fall, when gardeners are not buying and the leftover plants are on sale.

Raspberries are invasive weeds which have the habit of producing delicate flavored berries on their second year growth. The first year they grow green canes which are covered with bristles. If the plants are pruned back a little, the roots will send out runners even faster, to produce more raspberries. The second year the canes will look woody and will produce little white flowers (rose family, 5 petals) and then fruit. The two year canes are cut down each year and the green canes are thinned out (John 15:1-8). Raspberry cuttings are good for composting and for rabbit food. The leaves are considered medicinal for rabbits.

Once established, raspberries need to be thinned or they will crowd themselves out. I like them along a wall or against the garage, where they form a dense cover for birds and other animals. Raspberries like to be mulched and thinned out. They need water when they flower and fruit in the summer, but mulch will hold in the moisture and encourage the earthworm community. Raspberries need good drainage in the soil, and earthworms will tunnel channels for the water to drain away, yet hold moisture in the casts and organic material drawn down into the soil.

I once spotted a neighborhood cat in the raspberry canes, waiting in the shadows for birds to land on the lawn. I decided it was a good time to water the berries with the high powered patio cleaning attachment. The cat's aversion to water was greater than its attraction to birds.

Blackberries are another delicacy easily grown. Of all the foods converted from sunlight, surely blackberries are the best. They like good soil and mulch, plenty of sun, and enough moisture when flowering and fruiting. They are more likely to need support than raspberries.

Raspberries can be used to fill in a sunny area which would be covered with weeds and neglected otherwise. Blackberries can be used as an organic fence. Blackberry thorns are so effective that they seem to reach out and snag flesh and clothing. No one will go through a blackberry patch willingly a second time.

SIX

Gardening With Children

Sharing the garden with children is one of the great pleasures of planting and harvesting according to the principles of Creation. I cannot imagine being outside and having children walk past, void of curiosity. The younger they are, the more they want to know all about plants. They want to touch, smell, examine, and ask questions. Only a cad would say, "I'm too busy enjoying God's Creation to answer your questions."

Parents and grandparents who want their offspring to have a good understanding about science and the Christian faith can create a living laboratory in their yards. Jesus taught in parables, giving earthy examples about the Kingdom of God. A modest garden is filled with parables about growth, Creation, God's design and purpose, order, discipline, and beauty.

The five children of our neighbor in Columbus came over often to ask about our roses and the garden. When they saw I had a large area to seed, they demanded to be hired "for money and treats." All five grabbed the seed packets and planted with abandon (Matthew 13). I had no idea which seeds were planted where, but we all had a lot of fun, capped with their well-earned salaries, cookies, and soda. Their father was a little embarrassed by their project, but I enjoyed it and the random harvest which followed in the fall.

Herbs: God's Weedy Medical Wonders

Of all the plants, herbs are generally the most interesting for children. They often have unusual textures and aromas, and few will be harmed by a child's touch. I grew violets, an herb, in the shade of our pine trees in Midland and hung a hammock between the trees. Children played and rested in the hammock, trampling the violets flat. Parents would say, "Oh dear, we have ruined your plants." But I would assure them, "The violets will be back in less than a week." And they were. The flowers can be floated in punch for decoration or eaten in salads.

Almost all flowers and vegetables do well with rich soil, but many herbs not only tolerate poor soil but thrive in it. What Rodale calls "nature's miracle plants," we call God's weedy medical wonders. They can be called weeds because they grow in abundance in the wild and are often considered a nuisance in the garden. I grew a beautiful mullein in my yard, on purpose, only to have my neighbor sniff over the fence, "What is that?"

I said, "It's a mullein. Birds like to rest on them."

She deflected that comment by asking, "Isn't it a weed?"

When our son needed eye muscle surgery at the Cleveland Clinic, we did not object to the drug curare being used, even though it is derived from a weed growing in the jungles of South America.

Herbs are medical wonders because they build chemical factories which were valued in the past and are now being rediscovered. It is no surprise that the Greek word for sorcery is the root for our word pharmacy.[27] Common plants will manufacture substances which alleviate pain, cause pain, settle the stomach, induce vomiting, encourage hallucinations, heal babies, and cause abortions. Herbal knowledge was perverted for sorcery and witchcraft, but became the basis for the modern drug industry. Some of the claims about herbs today are perhaps overstated, but we can nevertheless be impressed that God created so many medicinal plants and made them so hardy that we can find them everywhere. When a plant has *officinalis* as part of its name, treat it with respect, because it is definitely an herb. But not all herbs have *officinalis* in their name.

The purpose of this chapter is not to practice medicine with herbs but to show how herbs can be an important part of the garden, a delight for children and adults. The Rodale definition of an herb is "a plant or plant part valued for its medicinal, savory, or aromatic qualities."[28] Since all things in Creation work together for His purpose, we can assume that God has appointed certain plants to benefit the natural order, even if we do not fully understand the complex relationships.

Garlic and Chives

Garlic is valued for its medicinal and aromatic qualities. I will not plant roses without garlic growing around each bush. If someone doubts that garlic produces powerful chemicals, let him leave a bag of freshly harvested bulbs in a sun-warmed car for several hours. When he climbs into the car filled with garlic fumes, as I did, let him imagine how the sensors of insects respond to the same aroma.

Garlic is supposed to make roses stronger, healthier, more aromatic, and less prone to insect damage. Natural insect repellents for plants are made with ground garlic in solution. I plant garlic all through the garden. One clove in the spring produces a bulb in the fall, while fall planted cloves produce in the spring. Garlic multiplies quickly. Many people now take garlic in pills or eat it raw simply for its health benefits.

Roses love garlic, and so does meat. People who cook with garlic will enjoy the flavor of garlic and its benefits. Roman soldiers ate garlic to make them stronger. Legions of garlic eating soldiers may have assumed wrongly that their weapons frightened their opponents.

Chives are closely related to garlic, so a rose gardener may want to plant chives around some bushes, as long as garlic is not already there. The chives will gradually spread and provide a green blanket, even if woody mulch is used. The chives can then be harvested many times over for use in salads and cooking.

Feverfew

Another companion for roses is feverfew, a prolific white flower which will seed itself once given a small start. The flowers grow around the bases of the rose and do not compete with the looks of the rose or the root system.

Rose

Roses themselves are herbs. Their fruit is called a hip, which is rich in vitamin C. Rosehip tea is a popular drink, if a little tart. Many vitamin C supplements are made up of rosehips, which Nostradamus used successfully in his days as a physician.

Rose petals can be used in foods. Dried, they are popular for scenting closets and dressers. Children like to collect and dry the petals. The older roses are more rugged and more aromatic. They are becoming popular for the advantages they have over their spoiled, fussy, and glamorous descendants, the hybrid teas.

Mullein

Mullein came to America as a garden plant and escaped. It is a two-year plant, so its first year is spent as a rosette of large velvety leaves on the ground. In its second year it sends up a leafy spike which flowers and bears seed. It does so well in sandy soil that it could be called the state flower of Michigan. Birds enjoy sitting on its branches.

Mullein was brought over for a variety of medicinal purposes, but it can be a good accent plant in the garden. *Horticulture* magazine, a high-

Let's take the scenic route.

toned periodical for sophisticated gardeners, published a feature article on them.[29] In flower, mullein looks like gigantic gladioli. Their seeds can be ordered from:

Thompson and Morgan
P. O. Box 1308
Jackson, NJ 08527-0308.

Thompson and Morgan have an attractive catalog with many exotic seeds. Reading it is an education for the novice or veteran. The photos make it instructive for children as well.

Comfrey

Comfrey is called knitbone for its reputed healing powers and ass ear for its appearance. It is a member of the borage family, which means that it grows with abandon. The young leaves may be eaten, but I have never been overly tempted. Our pet rabbits ate it, but I do not remember them eating it as readily as other herbs and wildflowers, such as roses, raspberries, and shepherd's purse. Children may want to grow some comfrey and gather leaves for the compost.

Borage

A much smaller relative of comfrey is borage, small enough to grow indoors in pots, so prolific in feeding bees with its flowers that it is nicknamed "bee bread." It is hardy and self-seeds as easily as feverfew.

Borage flowers are pink and blue, ideal for adding to salads. The leaves have a slight cucumber flavor. It is said to treat depression. A Latin poem says:

Ego borago
Gaudia semper ago.
I, borage,
Will always give you courage.

Borage flowers, along with other edible flowers, can be dipped in raw egg white, then sugar. They can then be eaten alone or added as edible decorations to ice cream, cake, or both. Most children will not admit to liking salad, but they will like gathering flowers to eat in their salad.[30]

Salad Burnet

Another good herb for salads is salad burnet. Like borage, it mimicks the flavor of cucumbers. It thrives in poor soil, while borage enjoys rich soil. The plant delighted our bunnies, which caused my wife to refuse it in her salad. Soon after, we went to an expensive French restaurant to try to spend all the money which a liberal magazine gave me for reprinting an article of mine critical of liberalism. On the menu was a very expensive salad which featured salad burnet. I wondered aloud why a classy joint would sell bunny food. Chris, my wife got the point, but hushed me up. Animals and humans alike enjoyed salad burnet from then on.

Purslane

Purslane was brought to Europe for salads and escaped, as it did in America. It seems to like corn patches especially well, but I have found it growing in planters on city streets and along the masonry wall at the New Ulm parsonage.

People go nuts over the plants which occupy open patches of soil, but those plants cannot compete with normal plants. Pulling up witch (or quack) grass, which has wire roots attached to the center of the earth, is much harder than ignoring it, mulching, and avoiding bare patches. Likewise, purslane will never go away, so it might as well be eaten.

When I returned from a vacation, purslane had grown from a creeping fleshy plant to a four foot monster, finding an open place in the mulch and feeding off pure compost in my corn patch. I yanked it out for a while, then concluded it was a guardian of the soil, just like the book said. Extra mulch kept it down.

Purslane is fine to eat raw in the garden. It has no special virtues. If it took $100 worth of fertilizer to keep it alive for one season, people would probably eat it all the time and try to find ways to make it grow better.

Tansy and Rue

Tansy, also known as stinking willie and button weed, will never go away once established. It was once used in cooking and to repel flies. It is also used to make the liqueur Chartreuse. Its aroma is interesting, something like Vicks Vap-o-Rub. Children like to crush herbs and then identify the smell.

Rue is also supposed to repel insects. It is called the herb-of-grace because of its use in medieval church services, to sprinkle holy water on the congregation.

Dill and Queen-Ann's-Lace

Few children need long to figure out the name of dill seed when they crush it in their hands. "It smells just like a pickle!" Dill is a little sluggish to grow the first time it is seeded, but from then on it seeds itself with relish. The leaves and seeds can be used in many ways in cooking. The seed heads look like tiny umbrellas, so they are called umbellifers (umbrella carriers). All their cousins have the same umbrella seed heads (parsley, carrot, fennel, and queen-ann's-lace).

Queen-ann's-lace (wild carrot) is not an herb, but it is interesting for a number of reasons. Its flowers seem to have a bug stuck on them. God created them that way to attract other insects. Evolutionists would need to claim that queen-ann's-lace without the bug spot did not succeed, while the spotted variety flourished. However, dill has no spot and seeds itself so well that one packet of dill seed is enough for ever and ever, Amen.

Queen-ann's-lace is given its name because of the queen who sewed so diligently. Once she pricked herself with a needle, hence the dark spot on the flower.

The flower attracts good insects, bees as well as lace wings, so it is good to have some growing in the garden.

Parsley

Another two year plant is parsley, which is strong-flavored but nutritious. Parsley demands rich soil and is slow to germinate. It attracts the black swallowtailed butterfly.

I had to mention parsley because I had such a beautiful stand of it, growing on compost made from upside-down sod dug from the front yard. The herbalist who gave me a start in herbs called her business The Parsley Patch until another business registered under that name. The herbalist sold to the expensive French restaurant, mentioned earlier, but had no parsley one week, due to rabbit predation. I was able to donate perfect parsley to The Parsley Patch and became insufferable for several weeks.

Parsley will self-seed the second year and should stay in business if the rabbits leave it alone. Some argue that one should grow catnip (a mint) to attract cats to repel rabbits.

Mints

One unpopular mint goes by many names: jill-over-ground, creeping charlie, etc. The stem is square and the leaves have a mint aroma. Mints spread through the roots, love good soil, and become very invasive in time. Children learn to identify mints by their square stems and their distinct aroma.

If someone really wants to grow a mint, he should make sure it is totally enclosed and unable to escape. It flowers constantly, attracting bees. The growth gets coarse and the aroma tiresome in time. Catnip is fun for those who have cats, since the felines go crazy over it.

Sunflower

Sunflowers have been chopped out of fields as weeds and grown as oil and seed plants. The secret to growing truly entertaining sunflowers is to buy the Russian mammoth variety, and have a contest to see who has the biggest seed head at the end. Sunflowers demand lots of water and very rich soil. They turn sunlight into energy even more efficiently than corn.   A row of sunflowers should have the soil dug down to several feet and replaced with compost and old manure. They will do better with a thick blanket of grass clippings as mulch. Sunflowers will droop as soon as they are low on water.

Squirrels will eat the blossom before seeds are formed. If several are grown, one flower might be taken by squirrels while the rest go to seed. We looked at the garden one day and saw a sunflower swaying wildly. A squirrel was on it upside-down, eating and swinging at the same time.

Birds will eat the seed when the heads start to fill out and dry. Not

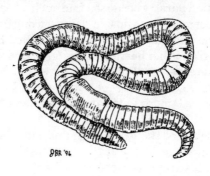

8BR '96

128

much damage is done, and the purpose should be to feed them anyway.

Many times I have distributed a certain number of sunflower seeds to each child in church, with instructions to plant them and bring the results to church later in the summer, once the seed heads are formed. The purpose is to illustrate the parable of the sower in Matthew 13.

True to form, one child ate his seeds, so they were never planted. Others had various problems. But the ones which germinated and grew produced hundreds and hundreds of seed from one seed. The people in the congregation saw tiny packets of seeds go home with the children, but platter-sized seed heads came back in a few months. We had no way of knowing on the first Sunday which seed would actually turn into a super-spirograph of seeds.

> And he spake many things unto them in parables, saying, Behold, a sower went forth to sow; {4} And when he sowed, some seeds fell by the way side, and the fowls came and devoured them up: {5} Some fell upon stony places, where they had not much earth: and forthwith they sprung up, because they had no deepness of earth: {6} And when the sun was up, they were scorched; and because they had no root, they withered away. {7} And some fell among thorns; and the thorns sprung up, and choked them: {8} But other fell into good ground, and brought forth fruit, some an hundredfold, some sixtyfold, some thirtyfold. (Matthew 13:3-8)

The great hymn writer and theologian, Martin Franzmann (1907-1976), wrote:

> Though some be snatched and some be scorched And some be choked and matted flat, The sower sows; his heart cries out, "Oh, what of that, and what of that?"

> Preach you the Word and plant it home And never faint; the Harvest Lord Who gave the sower seed to sow Will watch and tend his planted Word.

The sunflower itself is not one single flower but a complex flower. The bees work hard to pollinate the entire area. When the seeds form, one can see the same patterns formed by the child's toy, The Super Spirograph, which makes circles in a circle. Turning the seed head back and forth makes people gasp as they see the beauty of God's design and weigh the protein and vitamin feast in their own hands. Sunflower seeds are superstars in protein, phosphorous, iron, and vitamin A, with potassium and niacin as well. Their protein content, 25 percent, makes them equal to meat.

Sunflower stalks are woody when the flower is harvested, making them useful in compost. Placed in various locations in the compost, they will rot away and form air tunnels which will hasten the completion of the compost and decrease the need for turning the heap to give it air.

Periwinkle

I saw periwinkle under a tree and mentioned how much I liked it to the home owner, an accountant. "It's myrtle," he said crossly. Periwinkle is also called myrtle and sometimes vinca minor as well.

Periwinkle has been used as ground cover under trees, since it tolerates shade, and to hold steep slopes in place with its iron root system. The flowers are periwinkle blue or white. The plants are very expensive but fill in over time, especially if they are weighed down with rocks so they take root at the point where the plant touches the soil.

If possible, plant top grade daffodils first, before the periwinkle. The daffodils will bloom with the blue flowers seeming to form a starry background in the dense evergreen foliage.

Monarda: Bee Balm

Another plant with too many names is monarda, red bergamot, bee balm, or Oswego tea. The herb served as a substitute for tea after the Masonic Boston Tea Party. People grow it now to attract butterflies and hummingbirds. It is a small bush which can be purchased from a garden store. Children and adults love to watch butterflies, which are rare now, due to spraying insecticides instead of relying on birds and bats to feed on pests. The insect pests remain, but the butterflies and lady bugs are scarce.

Lobelia

Lobelia, or Indian tobacco, has medicinal substances which are being investigated. Those who love hummingbirds swear that their favorite bird is present the moment lobelias flower. Having a hummingbird and butterfly garden will provide hours of relaxation and enjoyment, as well as education for children.

CHILDREN'S GARDEN PROJECTS

I have described some garden projects aimed at children, who will enjoy studying books about these subjects if they have contact with the subject matter and a personal interest. Parents, teachers, and grandparents may want to pick some of the projects to do, asking the children which one seems most appealing. The local library often has fine children's books about nature. If the adults read the books with the children, everyone will learn at the same time.

1)   Each child has his own garden plot, which he will plant, take care of, and harvest on his own. Some easy plants to grow are: beans, lettuce, spinach, radishes, and gourds. They may want to build a bean or gourd teepee (see chapter six).

2)   Herb and wildflower identification. Instead of looking at odd plants as weeds, the children identify them and find out what value they have. Some common herbs found in backyards are: mullein, purslane, mint, dandelion, violet. Some wildflowers which may show up are: thistle, shepherd's purse, mallow, deadly nightshade, woody nightshade, goosefoot, and plantain.

3)   Backyard bird identification. Each child starts a life list of all the birds he has seen in his lifetime, just like adult bird watchers. Backyard birds will include bluejays, robins, various sparrows, starlings, grackles, crows, cardinals, and various finches.

4)   Bird feeding. Each child has his own bird feeder to maintain. Bird feeders do not have to be expensive store models, but leftover trays and dishes. The children study what birds like and try to supply as much as possible from leftovers: free suet from the butcher, bread crusts, stale cookies, popcorn. They also experiment with placement of the food: on the ground, nailed to the tree, on a table.

5)   Bird nest material. Children gather ingredients for birds to use in their nests: straw, drier lint, feathers, string, grass, twigs, and mud. They keep track of which materials are used and by what birds, if possible.

6) Bird baths. Various bird baths are set up in different locations and at different levels. Children study which birds favor one type of bath.

7) Squirrel feeder. An ear of field corn is placed on a spike near a window. When does the squirrel feed? How many feed from the same ear? How do they settle their territorial disputes? What do they do when humans are near the window? Do they beg for food when the cob is empty? The observations are written in a notebook.

8) Insect identification. A butterfly net can be fashioned from some nylon net, a wire hanger, and a wooden pole. To avoid stings from bees, insects are dumped into a glass jar for study. Using a basic insect guide from a bookstore or library, insects species are written down on the child's life list.

9) Beneficial insects. Praying mantis egg cases can be bought from

132

Gurney's or another supply house. The cases, which appear to be made from styrofoam, are tied to bushes, somewhat hidden from birds. When they hatch and grow, they are fun to study. Other beneficial insects to buy are: lace wings, lady bugs, and trichogramma wasps.

10) Spiders. Early in the morning, when dew is still on the ground, look for spider webs. The common garden spider should have a large web in a non-toxic garden. What is the purpose of the strange, irregular stitch pattern in the web? Does it ever change? How do spiders catch and eat their prey? How strong is the spider web? Do birds use spider web to construct their nests? Children may want to draw the spider and his web. A photograph of a dewy web is especially attractive.

11) Houses for birds, bats, and butterflies. Obtain a book on building bird, bat, and butterfly houses. If possible, buy or build a home for one of these beneficial creatures. The children should study what each creature does to benefit man, other animals, and plants. Bats are harmless and do not carry rabies more often than any other wild creature.

12) Moles. If the yard has mole runs, explore their pattern. Look for breathing holes. Examine the soft earth pushed out by the moles. Study books about them. What natural methods make them leave the yard? What does not work? (Water, for instance, since they swim like fish.) How many types of moles are there?

13) Nitrogen. How does God provide for the greening of His plants? Why is nitrogen so important to plants, animals, and humans? Why does a summer rain green up the lawn when hours of sprinkling will not?

14) Soil creatures. Each child draws up a list of all life in the soil of the backyard: fungus, bacteria, protozoa, sowbugs, pillbugs, millipedes, centipedes, springtails, mites, ants, earthworms, spiders, grubs, mice, voles, and moles. How does God arrange for all these forms of life to survive?

15) The rotting log. What happens when a log is left on the soil to rot? If God did not create the process of reduction, what would life be like? How many creatures are fed or sheltered by a rotting log.

16) Compost. The entire family starts a compost bin by enclosing an area at least 3 feet tall and 10 feet around. They study how a compost pile works

by drawing God's soil creatures into action. They form a strategy for using as much organic material as possible in their compost, including neighborhood leaves and grass. The younger children make sure the compost is kept damp during dry weather.

17) Field worm dig. Soil is turned over to look for field worms. Each shovel should have one worm. The worm is examined to find his/her main body parts and the bristles which help propel it. The parents or teacher discuss the earthworm's unique ability to improve and plow the soil.

18) Red wiggler buy. The family buys 1,000 red wigglers from an earthworm supplier. Some are placed near the compost pile (but not in a warm one) in bright sunlight. They will dig under quickly. Others are placed in the garden where the soil is rich or where mulch will feed the worms. The family then traces the spread of the red wigglers through the yard or studies the lack of progress.

19) Rabbits. If the children are serious about raising a rabbit, the proper materials are gathered to make a comfortable home for the rabbit. Red wiggler earthworms are placed under his cage to process the droppings, whether they fall on soil or into bins. How do we see the nitrogen cycle completed in feeding plants to the rabbits, who feed the earthworms, who feed the plants?

20) Leaves. The fall leaves are gathered, but not burned or bagged. Why do they make such a good insulating material around rose bushes? Why do they have the potential for adding minerals to the soil which other plants cannot add? How long do they take to compost? What will speed up their decomposition?

21) The moon. The more we study the moon, the more we see how God designed for us a night light for evening illumination (not too bright), and a powerful force in tides, thus setting up a complicated cycle of food for the oceans and areas where the ocean mixes with fresh water. It is fun to study the moon and its cycles.

22) The moon and weather. Does the moon affect the weather? Get a barometer and track how often a high pressure area coincides with a full moon, and how often rain follows a full moon. One junior high student prepared his own weather maps in color each day.

23) The stars. Each child should learn the major constellations and how to find the North Star. Binoculars are a good start in observing the sky, far more satisfying than the cracker jack telescopes which are often bought for Christmas presents. If a telescope is purchased, after getting full use of binoculars, buy one which is no smaller than a 6 inch reflector (which uses a mirror). Refractors (lens only) are expensive. *Astronomy* magazine is a good start on studying the skies.

THE MIGHTY EARTHWORM

God often uses the ordinary to make foolish the wisdom of the wise. In the earthworm we have a creature which is so common that we seldom think that our entire civilization turns on him. Without his work, our soil would be solid, sterile, lifeless, barren of vegetation, blown away by abrading winds, swept away by murderous floods. Our thankless civilization depends on his labors, not only for making the soil productive, but also for making it healthy, sweet, ready to give up its minerals to plants and ultimately to man.

Charles Darwin, a lapsed theology student, studied the earthworm for 40 years and drew the conclusion that the lowly digger of soil was responsible for burying rocks, boulders, and entire cities. Although floods and earthquakes have leveled great cities, no force on earth has made so many buildings disappear as the earthworm, displacing only a tiny bit of soil each day.

The earthworm is a world traveler as well as an embalmer of cities. He has hitched rides on the hooves of animals, sent his children across the ocean nestled in the seedlings of dreamy colonists, and brought soil fertility to areas where everything abounded except the work of the lumbricid.

While the earthworm was extending his benevolent reach across the globe, to make the Americas and New Zealand fertile, blind science was extending the influence of Darwin, who missed entirely the divine design and purpose of the earthworm: to improve the soil. Dismissing God by fiat, the new science proposed to kill all weeds, fertilize all crops, and gas all insects with manufactured chemicals. The initial results made people giddy with the hopes of progress, not knowing they had created an agricultural Tower of Babel.

The Dust Bowl showed farmers that the soil, created and sustained by God's creatures, could not be assaulted and exploited without a price.

The ocean of life in the soil was poisoned with the best of intentions, flailed by over-zealous plowing, and drained of its organic material. When the organic glue was gone, the soil left in great whirlwinds of darkness, grit, and woe.

I grew up on a steady diet of evolution, which was taught in subtle ways through many years of school. Most of the science information I receive today is still transmitted in the language of evolution, with certain concessions to the reality of design and purpose. The bird's feather and the human eye both defy a rationalistic answer, especially when seen through the eye of a microscope. However, almost all nature shows on TV, for instance, bow to Darwin at least once during the program. Most scientific journals also promote one and only one view of this universe, Darwin's. His philosophy is really antique now, based upon constant progress, imagining that man is always getter better, smarter, more self reliant and less religious.

As parents, pastors, and teachers, we owe it to our children to give them a proper understanding of God's Creation by observing it with them, by showing them what the Word of God teaches, and by sharing their great sense of wonder. We have, to help us teach, the greatest faculty ever assembled:

1) the earthworm and his colleagues in the soil;
2) the birds, bats, and butterflies;
3) the beneficial insects and their pesky relatives;

4) the cultivated and wild flowers;
5) the herbs and weeds;
6) the vegetables and fruits;
7) the moon, planets, and stars.

With us they sing:
> **Beautiful Savior, King of Creation,**
> **Son of God and Son of Man!**
> **Truly I'd love thee,**
> **Truly I'd serve thee,**
> **Light of my soul, my joy, my crown.**
> **Amen.**

Annotated Bibliography

Introduction

Faulkner, Edward. *Plowman's Folly*. Omaha: University of Omaha Press. 1943

Faulkner argued that green manure (a crop allowed to rot into the soil) could improve impossible soil without plowing, that plowing does nothing to improve the soil. No-till farming is now accepted, more than 50 years later. What does this say about the over use of roto-tillers in the garden?

Jackson, Gregory L. *Liberalism: Its Cause and Cure, The Poisoning of American Christianity and the Antidote*. Milwaukee: Northwestern Publishing House. 1991.

This book was written to explain why the majority of American ministers today, in the oldest denominations, deny the inerrancy of the Scriptures, the Virgin Birth of Christ, His atoning death and His bodily resurrection. The compromise of leading Evangelicals with the theory of evolution is discussed in chapter three: "The Mainline Churches and Evolution."

Menton, David. "Creation versus Evolution." *Lutheran Spokesman* magazine, 710 4th Avenue, Sleepy Eye, Minnesota, 56085, reprinted in *Christian News*.

Dr. Menton is a member of the Church of the Lutheran Confession and an associate professor of anatomy at the Washington University School of Medicine. As a scientist and a believer, he takes on the claims of evolution and defeats them.

Shewell-Cooper, Wilfred Edward. *Compost Gardening*. New York: Hafner Press. 1974

Shewell-Cooper's radical idea simplifies gardening. Compost should be used on top of the garden area as mulch rather than tilled into the soil. Earthworms will pull the compost into the soil without backbreaking labor for the gardener.

Sippert, Albert. *From Eternity to Eternity, A Treatise on the Origin and Destiny of All Things*. North Mankato: Sippert Publishing Company, 1989.
Pastor Sippert, Church of the Lutheran Confession, deals with the theory and evidence of evolution and counters with the Biblical doctrine of Creation. This popular book serves as a good introduction to the issues of Creation *versus* evolution.

Stout, Ruth. *How to Have a Green Thumb Without an Aching Back*. New York: Exposition Press. 1961.
Stout discovered by accident that mulching with hay would eliminate the need for tilling, fertilizing, and weeding. Through articles in *Organic Gardening* and several books, she convinced gardeners to make their compost on the spot, in the garden itself.

Biology of the Earthworm

Appelhof, Mary. *Worms Eat My Garbage*. Kalamazoo: Flower Press. 1982.
Appelhof has published an informative book about how to turn kitchen garbage into compost inside the house, using the manure worm.

Barrett, Thomas J. *Harnessing the Earthworm*. Ontario: Bookworm Publishing. 1976.
Barrett was a pioneer in using the earthworm to improve the soil. He wrote about his grandfather's farm, which used a gigantic earthworm composting pit to handle manure and renew the farm's soil—in the 1830's. His discussion of the British study of earthworms and Nile agriculture is most revealing.

Darwin, Charles. *The Formation of Vegetable Mould Through the Action of Worms With Observations on Their Habits*. Ontario: Bookworm Publishing. 1976. (First published in 1881)
Darwin's 40 years of observations are eloquently recorded in this classic work, little known outside the earthworm community. Darwin observed that earthworms create topsoil by excreting castings, but concentrated on their effect in burying buildings over time rather than in renewing the soil.

Edwards, C. A., and J. R. Lofty. *Biology of Earthworms*. Ontario: Bookworm Publishing. 1972.

This scientific work generally confirms the claims of popular, anecdotal books about earthworms.

Gaddie, Ronald E. and Donald E. Douglas, *Earthworms for Ecology and Profit*, two volumes. Ontario: Bookworm Publishing. 1977.

Gaddie went into raising earthworms after a back injury disabled him. His Bookworm Publishing is the source of many hard to find books on earthworms.

Rehwinkel, Alfred M. *The Flood in the Light of the Bible, Geology, and Archeology*. St. Louis: Concordia Publishing House. 1951.

Rehwinkel, a theology professor, studied science and found no contradiction between the global flood of the Scriptures and the physical evidence which remains. In his view, only the Flood explains a host of modern day problems, such as the Grand Canyon.

Gardening for the Benefit of Earthworms

Hopp, Henry. *What Every Gardener Should Know About Earthworms*. Charlotte, Vermont: Garden Way. 1978. Hopp pioneered the use of earthworms and wrote a concise account of their benefits.

Howard, Albert. *An Agricultural Testament*. New York: Oxford University Press. 1943.

Howard rediscovered the compost pile in his effort to make manure last longer in India. He combined manure with vegetation to stretch out supplies, resulting in a complex process which greatly improved crops. His study of the Hunza tribe's use of organic methods and their resultant health still has an impact today.

Johnston, Cecil. "The Wild World of Compost," *National Geographic*, volume 158, number 2, August, 1980, pp. 273-284. This is a vivid photographic essay which illustrates the life and death struggles of soil creatures in a compost pile.

King, F. H. *Farmers of Forty Centuries*. Emmaus: Rodale Press. 1911. King studied the peasant agricultural methods of Japan, China, and

Korea, showing how the farmers were able to use the same land for productive crops for 4,000 years by recycling all organic materials into the soil.

Minnich, Jerry, et al. *The Rodale Guide to Composting*. Emmaus: Rodale Press. 1979. Few books can add to the information supplied by Minnich. Ingredients good for composting, their chemical make-up, and the benefits of using them are all explained clearly. Various methods of composting are discussed, along with plans for kinds of compost bins and piles. Composting with earthworms is given 15 pages.

Minnich, Jerry. *The Earthworm Book*. Emmaus: Rodale Press. 1977.
    This is a valuable companion to *The Rodale Guide to Composting*, covering raising earthworms, gardening and farming with earthworms, and raising them for bait. Minnich argues for a causal relationship between the abundance of lumbricid earthworms and the growth of civilization in those areas.

Voisin, Andre. *Better Grassland Sward*. London: Crosby, Lockwood, and

Fiacre, Patron Saint of Gardeners, Contemplates an Earthworm

Sons. 1960.

Voisin caused a sensation when he challenged assumptions about the soil and productivity. His book devotes seven chapters to: lazy and active earthworms, effects of fertilizers on earthworms, white clover and earthworms, the quality of grassland depending on the number and quality of earthworms, "the European earthworm conquers New Zealand," earthworms and continental drift, and "the earthworm, creator of civilizations."

Garden Ecology

Cocannouer, Joseph A. *Weeds - Guardians of the Soil*. New York: Devid-Adair. 1950.

This revolutionary book shows how valuable weeds can be: serving as companion plants, trapping insects, renewing soil, pumping nutrients from the subsoil, and feeding the compost pile.

Courtenay, Booth and James H. Zimmerman. *Wildflowers and Weeds*, A Guide in Full Color. New York: Van Nostrand Reinhold. 1972.

Weeds and wildflowers are grouped by color, making them easy to identify.

Gillespie, Janet. *Peacock Manure and Marigolds*. New York: Ballantine Books. 1964.

Gillespie explores the value of old-fashioned garden remedies in contrast with the use of manufactured toxins.

Harrison, George. *The Backyard Bird Watcher*. New York: Simon and Schuster. 1979.

Harrison gives excellent advice on attracting and housing backyard birds.

Harrison, Kit and George. *America's Favorite Backyard Birds*. New York: Simon and Schuster. 1983.

The Harrisons describe the common birds, their habits, and their value to us.

Heidcamp, Arnette. *A Hummingbird in My House: The Story of Squeak*. New York: Crown Publishers.

Heidcamp's first hummingbird boarder was a male ruby-throat. Her photos and personal experiences are great for the amateur bird watcher who wants to understand hummers.

_____. *Rosie, My Rufous Hummingbird*. New York: Crown Publishers. 1995.
    Heidcamp's second hummingbird boarder, a female rufous, is portrayed so well in photos and words that it is sad to see her set free at the end.

Hylton, William H., ed. *The Rodale Herb Book*. Emmaus: Rodale Press. 1974.
    Full descriptions of all herbs, how they can be used and grown, make this book an excellent resource.

Kanable, Ann. *Raising Rabbits*. Emmaus: Rodale Press. 1977.
    Lovable rabbits are the best pets a gardener can have, and this book will make raising them easy.

Larkcom, Joy. *The Salad Garden*. New York: The Viking Press. 1984.
    All the possibilities for growing a vast number of plants for salads are shown with vivid photos and illustrations.

Madson, John. *Where the Sky Began, Land of the Tallgrass Prairie*. Boston: Houghton-Mifflin. 1982.
    Reading about the ecology of the prairie, now mostly lost, will help the gardener appreciate the animals, plants, and soil in his own backyard.

Minnich, Jerry. *Gardening for Maximum Nutrition*. Easy Ways to Double the Nutritional Value of Your Backyard Garden. Emmaus: Rodale Press. 1983.
    Gardeners should consult this book when they plan which vegetables to grow.

Riotte, Louise. *Carrots Love Tomatoes*. Charlotte: Garden Way. 1975.
    Companion planting reduces pests and benefits the health of the plants. Each plant is discussed alphabetically, in terms of good and bad companions.

_____. *Roses Love Garlic*. Charlotte: Garden Way. 1983.
    Riotte concentrates on flowers in this volume.

Swain, Roger B. *Earthly Pleasures, Tales from a Biologist's Garden*. New

York: Charles Scribner's Sons. 1981.

Swain's entertaining essays describe such mundane but significant matters as the dungbeetle in Australia, the ripening of a tomato, and building beehives.

Wallace, Dan, ed. *Getting the Most from Your Garden*. Emmaus: Rodale Pres. 1980.

Wallace describes intensive gardening methods and companion planting, plus many useful tips in altering the garden's environment for better production.

Yepsen, Roger, ed. *The Encyclopedia of Natural Insect and Disease Control*. Emmaus: Rodale Press. 1984.

Gorgeous closeups in color of insect pests and plant diseases will motivate the reader to try natural controls designed by God.

SOURCES

Birds

Tips about rare birds and backyard birds abound in:

Bird Watcher's Digest
P. O. Box 110
Marietta OH 45750
Phone: 800-879-2473

Fascinating hummingbird books with color photos can be ordered from:

Arnette Heidcamp
P. O. Box 595
Glasco NY 12432

Books and Periodicals

Conservative books can be ordered from:

Church of the Lutheran Confession Book House
501 Grover Road
Eau Claire WI 54701-7199
Phone: 715-836-6623

Three magazines designed to promote the doctrine of Creation are written
from the Evangelical or Reformed point of view:

Creator
PO Box 785
Arvada CO 80001-0785

Discovery
Apologetics Press
230 Landmark Drive
Montgomery AL 36117
Phone: 1-800-234-8558

Our World
Creation Resources Trust
Mead Farm, Downhead
West Camel, Yeovil
Somerset England BA22 7RQ

The best known Creation association is also Reformed:

Institute for Creation Research
PO Box 2667
El Cajon CA 92021-0667
ICR sponsors a graduate school as well as publishing articles, books, and videos on the topic of Creation.

Organic Gardening magazine and dozens of books about composting, soil, pests, and gardening can be ordered from:

Rodale Press
Emmaus, PA 18098
1-800-666-2206

Bulbs

By far, the best provider of fall and spring bulbs, with a catalog which makes *National Geographic* look cheap, is Dutch Gardens. Their group orders are handled extremely well. Bulbs which do not grow are replaced free, if the receipt is kept.

Dutch Gardens
P. O. Box 200
Adelphia, NJ 07710
Phone: 908-780-2713
Fax: 908-780-7720.

Earthworms

President Jimmie Carter's cousin sells earthworms and mealy bugs:

Carter Fishworm
Farm Plains GA 31780

Books and worms can be ordered from:

Shields
Box 669-C
Eagle River WI 54521

Ron Gaddie publishes books and sells worms:

Bookworm Publishing
P. O. Box 655
Ontario CA 91761

Especially for Children

Ranger Rick magazine, wildlife essays, projects, and photos for younger children.

National Wildlife Federation
8925 Leesburg Pike
Vienna VA 22180

Gurney's seed catalog, with lots of unusual plants and beneficial insects. Their worms for sale must be gold plated.

Gurney's Seed and Nursery
110 Capital Street
Yankton, SD 57079
Phone: 605-665-1671

Fruit

Miller Nurseries
5060 West Lake Road
Canandaigua NY 14424
Phone: 800-836-9630

Stark Brothers
Louisiana MO 63353
Phone: 800-325-4180

Plants

One of the most attractive and educational catalogs comes from:

Wayside Gardens
Hodges SC 29695-0001
Phone: 800-845-1124

Roses

This catalog used to be the most fun to read, with sarcastic comments about certain roses.

Fred Edmunds
6235 SW Kahle Road
Wilsonville OR 97070
Phone:503-682-1476
Fax: 503-682-1275

Unfortunately, the author is not related to the largest grower of roses in America. They offer tree roses and many types of old roses, but their bulbs are overpriced.

Jackson and Perkins
P. O. Box 1028
Medford OR 97501
Phone: 800-292-4769
Fax: 800-242-0329

It often pays to buy plants which are used to cold weather, if one wants to garden in the north. One such supplier is:

Sam Kedem Greenhouse and Nursery
7874 165th Street East
Hastings MN 55033
Phone: 612-437-7516

Seeds

Burpee
300 Park Ave
Warminister PA 18991-0001
Phone: 800-888-1447

Jung Quality Seeds
335 S. High St.
Randolph WI 53957-0001
Phone: 800-247-5864

Park's
Cokesbury Road
Greenwood SC 29647-0001
Phone: 800-845-3369

Stokes
P. O. Box 548
Buffalo NY 14240-0548
Phone: 716-695-6980

Unusual Seeds

Reading this catalog is an education, since it is so well illustrated and filled with so many interesting seeds.
Thompson and Morgan
P. O. Box 1308
Jackson NJ 08527-0308
Phone: 800-274-7333

1. Jerry Minnich, *The Earthworm Book*, Emmaus: Rodale Press, 1977, P. 66.

2. *Ibid.*, p. 58.

3. Thomas Barrett, *Harnessing the Earthworm*, Ontario: 1976, pp. 25-28.

4. Minnich, *op. cit.*, p. 57.

5. *Ibid.*, pp. 59-64.

6. Andre Voisin, *Better Grassland Sward*, London, 1960, p. 290. Emphasis in the original.

7. *The Formation of Vegetable Mould*, Ontario: Bookworm Publishing, 1976, p. 50.

8. Barrett, *op. cit.*, p. 50.

9. *Ibid.*, p. 9.

10. Darwin, *op. cit.*, p. 12.

11. Minnich, *op. cit.*, p. 77.

12. Ronald Gaddie, Sr., and Donald Douglas, *Earthworms for Ecology and Profit, II*, Ontario: Bookworm Publishing, 1977, p. 73.

13. *Ibid.*, p. 75.

14. C. A. Edwards and J. R. Lofty, *Biology of Earthworms*, Ontario: Bookworm Publishing, 1976, p. 161.

15. Henry Hopp, *What Every Gardener Should Know about Earthworms*, 1978, p. 31.

16. Minnich, *op. cit.*, p. 115.

17. *Ibid.*, p. 116.

18. Consider the following schedule as an outline of work which can be done throughout the year.

Fall Work
1) Mow leaves onto flower beds.
2) Cover garden with grass clippings and mowed leaves.
3) Hold winter mulch in place with branches, if possible.
4) Order and plant fall bulbs.
5) Set up compost bins for leftover leaves and garden refuse.
6) Order and plant raspberries and blackberries.
7) Order roses.
8) Start spinach, then cover with leaves.

Winter Work
1) Feed suet to insect loving birds.
2) Buy a bird bath warmer and use in bird bath.
3) Feed field corn to squirrels, black oil sunflower seeds to birds and squirrels.

5) Order seeds.
6) Read gardening books and dream.

Early Spring Work

1) Enjoy hardy bulbs bloom.
2) Remove covering from spinach. Eat and brag.
3) Plant peas.
4) Keep birds fed and bathed. Gather twine, twigs, feathers, lint, and mud for their nests.
5) Order tender bulbs and asparagus.
6) Distribute compost. Start new compost.

Spring

1) Plant beans, corn, asparagus, tomatoes.
2) Plant tender bulbs.
3) Plant roses.
4) Prune blackberries and raspberries to force some growth.
5) Mulch with grass clippings and compost.
6) Cut back on bird feeding, but keep plenty of clean water in the bird bath. Use the suet when planting roses (an old wives' tale).
7) Enjoy perfect spinach.

Summer

1) Compost the pea vines and plant scarlet runner beans for the hummingbirds. Plant lobelia and monards.
2) Water when necessary. Try to gather and store rain water.
3) Enjoy the tender bulbs and roses blooming.
4) Mulch with grass clippings, pulled weeds, and compost.
5) Make friends with one horse owner or rabbit breeder.
6) Thin beets, carrots, swiss chard. Eat same.
7) Take notes on what worked and what did not.

Late Summer

1) Listen to the wails and complaints of those who did not garden according to the principles of Creation. Drought will kill their plants and boost their weeds.
2) Start harvesting the vegetables.
3) Plan on protecting plants which are vulnerable to frost.
4) Make compost or manure tea. Keep the roses mulched, watered, and fed.

Easy Compost Bin

1) Buy 10 feet of chicken wire or snow fence.
2) Form a circle.
3) Fill with leaves, grass, garden plants, soil, and manure.
4) Keep as damp as a wrung out sponge.
5) Move garbage can every few months.

19. John Madson, *Where the Sky Began, Land of the Tallgrass Prairie*, Boston: Houghton Mifflin, 1982, p. 30.

20. *Ibid.*, p. 30.

21. *National Geographic* (August, 1980) offers an excellent expedition into "The Wild World of Compost," by Cecil Johnson, pp. 273-284.

22. John Madson, Where the Sky Began, *Land of the Tallgrass Prairie*, Boston: Houghton Mifflin, 1082, p. 114.

23. The complete story is told in *Angel Joy*, available from Martin Chemnitz Press.

24. Matthias Claudius, 1740-1815, Hymn #362, *Lutheran Book of Worship*.

25. Heaven and earth shall pass away, but my words shall not pass away. (Matthew 24:35)

26. *Gardening for Maximum Nutrition*, Emmaus: Rodale Press, 1983, p. 41.

27. One of the works of the flesh in Galatians 5 is sorcery, the Greek word which is the root for pharmacy.

28. William H. Hylton, ed., *The Rodale Herb Book*, Emmaus: Rodale Press, 1974, p. 23.

29. Ann Lovejoy, "Inspired by Verbascums, The Hardy Mulleins Reach New Heights in the Border," *Horticulture*, August/September, 1995, pp. 30-34.

30. The following plants can be used in salads, many of them throughout the summer:
1) Spinach
2) Edible pod peas
3) Lettuce
4) Salad burnet
5) Borage
6) Beet greens
7) Swiss chard
8) Collards
9) Tomatoes
10) Chives
11) Broccoli
12) Cabbage

32. Some butterfly plants for the garden are:
1) Butterfly bush
2) Hollyhock
3) Milkweed
4) Mint
5) Queen-Anne's-Lace
6) Butterly weed
7) Dandelion
8) Yarrow

33. Those who want to attract hummingbirds by plants alone, without fussing with feeders, should grow:
1) Scarlet runner beans
2) Monarda or bee balm
3) Lobelia
4) Trumpet vine
5) Trumpet bush
6) Butterfly bush
7) Fuchsia
They should also have a bird bath, or even better, a small fountain which sprays water.

Recipe

Asparagus with Tomato/Basil Vinaigrette

2 Tbls. Coarsely chopped fresh basil
2 Tbls. olive oil
2 Tbls. cider vinegar
1/2 tsp. salt
1/4 tsp. sugar
1/8 tsp. pepper
1 pound fresh asparagus
1/3 cup finely chopped tomatoes

To make vinaigrette: combine chopped basil, olive oil, vinegar, salt, sugar and pepper in a jar; cover tightly and shake vigorously. Set vinaigrette mixture aside.

Snap off tough ends of asparagus. Remove scales with knife or vegetable peeler, if desired. Place in a vegetable steamer over boiling water (or in boiling water if you do not have a vegetable steamer). Cover and steam approximately 3-5 minutes, or until crisp-tender (you can just begin to smell the asparagus). Drain.

Arrange asparagus on a serving platter. Sprinkle with chopped tomato. Drizzle vinaigrette mixture over asparagus. Serve warm or at room temperature.

NOTE: This can also be made with broccoli, when asparagus is not available. Particularly if you make it in the winter time, be sure to use a tomato which has not been refrigerated.

Prefer to use your credit card?
1-573-237-3110

Fax: (573)237-3858
E-MAIL: OTTEN@AOL.COM
Or Return To: Lutheran News, 3277 Boeuf Lutheran Rd, New Haven, MO 63068

☐ My check, money order or cash is enclosed.

☐ Please charge $ _____ to my:

MasterCard ☐   Visa ☐

Card # _____ - _____ - _____ - _____

Exp. Date _____ / _____

Signature _____

Daytime Phone (___) _____

Quantity	Description	Price	Total
_____	Catholic, Lutheran, Protestant	$11.95	_____
_____	Liberalisn: Cause and Cure	$8.95	_____
_____	Angel Joy	$7.99	_____
_____	Wormhaven Gardening Book	$9.95	_____
		Items Total	_____
	Shipping (10% of Items Total)		_____
		Grand Total	_____